The Civil War: Essential Histories

The Civil War

Gettysburg and Other Eastern Battles 1863–1865

Robert O'Neill, Series Editor; and Robert K. Krick

This edition published in 2011 by:

The Rosen Publishing Group, Inc.
29 East 21st Street
New York, NY 10010

Library of Congress Cataloging-in-Publication Data

O'Neill, Robert John.
The Civil War: Gettysburg and other Eastern battles, 1863–1865 / Robert O'Neill, Robert K. Krick.
p. cm.—(The Civil War: Essential histories)
Includes bibliographical references and index.
ISBN 978-1-4488-0388-0 (library binding)
1. United States—History—Civil War, 1861–1865—Campaigns—Juvenile literature. 2. East (U.S.)—History, Military—19th century—Juvenile literature. 3. United States—Politics and government—1861–1865—Juvenile literature. I. Krick, Robert K. II. Title.
E470.2.K57 2011
973.7'3—dc22

2010004633

Manufactured in the United States of America

CPSIA Compliance Information: Batch #S10YA: For further information, contact Rosen Publishing, New York, New York, at 1-800-237-9932.

On the cover: Portrait of Ulysses S. Grant. (Smithsonian National Portrait Gallery)

Contents

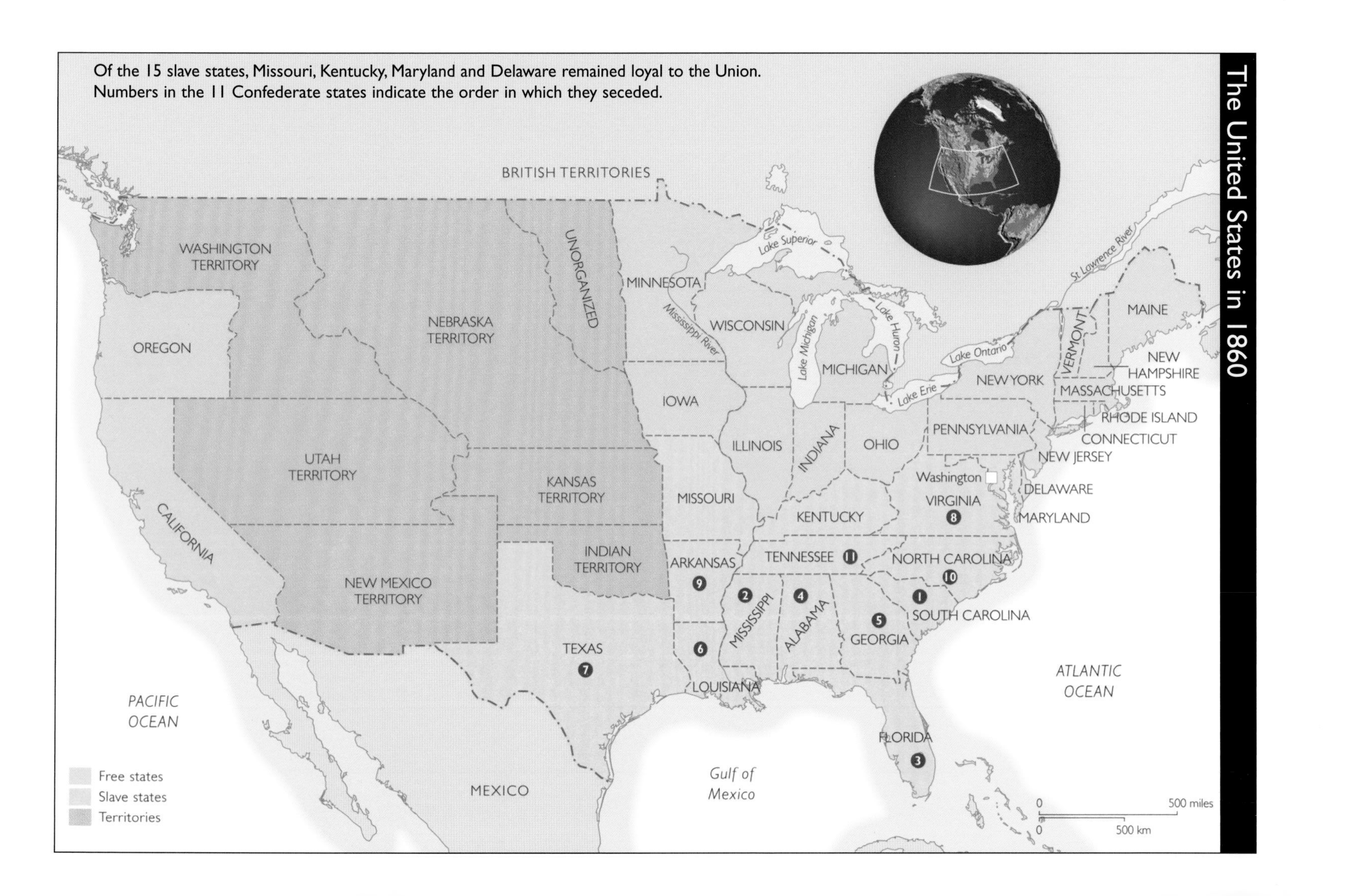

The United States in 1860

Of the 15 slave states, Missouri, Kentucky, Maryland and Delaware remained loyal to the Union. Numbers in the 11 Confederate states indicate the order in which they seceded.

Introduction

Robert Penn Warren, Pulitzer Prize winner and American Southerner, has suggested that the Civil War rivets the attention of readers because of the striking human images it offers for contemplation—"a dazzling array of figures, noble in proportion yet human, caught out of Time as in a frieze, in stances so profoundly touching or powerfully mythic that they move us in a way no mere consideration of 'historical importance' ever could." Most of those towering figures who carry a special aura functioned in the war's Eastern Theater, which is the focus of this volume. Lee, Jackson, Grant, and others of the American soldiers who fought that war continue to fascinate modern students.

The Essential Histories series divides the story of the American Civil War into four volumes. The rupture of the United States into two nations in 1861, detailed in *The Civil War: Bull Run and Other Eastern Battles 1861–May 1863*, by Gary Gallagher, led to a vast internecine war. Hundreds of thousands of young men eagerly embraced the adventure of war. They joined volunteer units near their homes and cheerfully, innocently, headed away to what seemed surely to be a short, clean conflict. It would end, they felt certain, in victory for whichever of the contending sides they embraced. The frolicsome aspect of war dissipated in the intense mayhem along Bull Run, on the plains of Manassas, in July 1861. For months thereafter, thousands of boys in both armies died of disease. Many of the rustic youngsters-turned-soldiers had never been far from rural homes and they fell prey in droves to common childhood diseases such as measles.

Gallagher, *The Civil War*, presents the story of the first half of the war in Virginia. After a relatively quiet first year of the war, the spring of 1862 ushered in months of steady campaigning in Virginia and Maryland, across the narrow swath of country between the contending capital cities of Washington, DC, and Richmond, Virginia. General Robert E. Lee assumed command of the Confederate Army of Northern Virginia on June 1, 1862, and with it drove the besieging Federal Army of the Potomac away from Richmond. During the 11 succeeding months, Lee steadily defeated an array of opposing generals: George B. McClellan, John Pope, Ambrose E. Burnside, and Joseph Hooker. The arenas in which Lee conquered that succession of enemies are among the most famous in American military history: the Seven Days' Campaign, Second Manassas (or Bull Run), Antietam, Fredericksburg, and Chancellorsville.

This second volume covers the war in the Eastern Theater from June 1863 to the surrender at Appomattox in April 1865. In the aftermath of Chancellorsville, the war in Virginia was about to undergo a fundamental change in tenor. The enormous Northern advantages in industrial might and population numbers would affect operations. With his invaluable lieutenant, "Stonewall" Jackson, dead, Lee would find his options narrowed. Hoping to retain the initiative, Lee grasped the momentum offered by Chancellorsville and surged northward into enemy territory. When he returned after Gettysburg, the nature of the war in Virginia would trend steadily away from Confederate opportunities, and toward eventual Unionist victory.

The great Battle of Gettysburg opened this second phase of the story. From Wilderness and Spotsylvania Court House the next spring, the contending armies moved to an extended siege of Petersburg, and eventually to the Confederate surrender at Appomattox. The Confederate Army of Northern Virginia

ON THE CONFEDERATE LINE OF BATTLE "WITH FATE AGAINST THEM."

FROM THE PAINTING BY GILBERT GAUL.

(Public domain)

followed General Robert E. Lee through the entire period. That army's sturdy, if ill-led, counterpart was the Union Army of the Potomac. General George G. Meade took over the Army of the Potomac just a few hours before its great victory at Gettysburg, and retained that command to the end of the war. The arrival of the commander of all Union armies, General U. S. Grant, in the field near the Army of the Potomac in the spring of 1864 overshadowed Meade and he never has received the immense credit that he deserves for winning the war.

Wars invariably generate momentum of their own, leading to results that neither side envisioned, or would have tolerated, at the outset. By 1864 the old-fashioned war of 1861–63, caparisoned with the trappings of antique chivalry, had given way to what aptly has been called "the first modern war." Railroads for the first time played an essential role. Industrial and mechanical might weighed in as heavily as tactical prowess and strategic skill. Troops who had been scornful of earthworks in 1861 frantically dug dirt in 1864 at every opportunity, to protect themselves. Perhaps most significantly, most in the modern vein, civilians and their property became the targets of military power.

As have most attempts to win independence and freedom over the centuries, the efforts to create a Confederate nation had to rely upon wearing down the will of their foe. Southerners had nothing remotely like the means to (or any interest in) subjugate their opponents as a vassal state; they merely longed to be let alone. Perhaps the most important day in the second half of the war, therefore, was November 8, 1864, when the Northern populace voted a second term for President Abraham Lincoln—who had been certain a few weeks earlier that he would lose. With the aggressive war party still in power in the North, determined to win the war, Confederates had no hope of beating an enemy with thrice the military population and virtually all of the continent's industrial capacity.

The surrender at Appomattox followed inevitably, leaving behind legendary battles and leaders who remain among the most-studied military topics in the English language. The war also left a ghastly harvest of more than 620,000 dead men in its wake, by far the largest proportional loss in American history; freed several million black men and women from slavery; and created an unmistakable watershed in United States history.

From June 1862 to May 1863, Confederate General Robert E. Lee had steadily defeated an array of opposing Federal generals. (Author's collection)

Chronology

1863 **May 10** Confederate General "Stonewall" Jackson dies
June 9 Cavalry battle at Brandy Station
June 14–15 Second Battle of Winchester
June 28 General George G. Meade replaces Joseph Hooker in command of the Federal Army of the Potomac in the midst of the campaign, just before the war's largest battle
July 1–3 Battle of Gettysburg
July 13–14 Lee's Confederates recross the Potomac River into Virginia, ending the main phase of the Gettysburg campaign. At the same time, frenzied mobs in New York City riot in opposition to conscription, killing or wounding hundreds of victims, many of them black citizens resented as a visible cause of the war and the draft.
September 8–14 Lee detaches General Longstreet with one-third of the army's infantry to go west and reinforce Confederate operations in Georgia and Tennessee. Meade moves south against Lee, but only heavy skirmishing results.
October 14 Battle of Bristoe Station
November 7 Battle of Rappahannock Station
November 19 President Lincoln delivers the Gettysburg Address
November 26–December 2 Battle of Mine Run
November 8 President Lincoln issues a Proclamation of Amnesty and Reconstruction, offering pardons to any Confederate willing to take an oath of allegiance

1864 **March 9** Grant is commissioned lieutenant-general, to command all Federal armies. He would make his headquarters with the Army of the Potomac, and soon exert virtually direct command over it.
May 4–6 Battle of the Wilderness
May 8–21 Battle of Spotsylvania Court House
May 11 Battle of Yellow Tavern; General J. E. B. Stuart is mortally wounded and dies the next day
May 15 Battle of New Market
May 23–27 Battle of the North Anna River
June 1–3 Battle of Cold Harbor
June 5 Battle of Piedmont
June 12 Army of the Potomac starts move to cross James River
June 15–18 Opening engagements around Petersburg, while Confederate General Jubal Early arrives near Lynchburg to launch his long and crucial campaign in the Shenandoah Valley
June 22–23 Battle for the Weldon Railroad near Petersburg
July 9 Battle of Monocacy
July 11–12 Early's Confederates stand on the outskirts of Washington; President Lincoln comes under long-range fire
July 24 Second Battle of Kernstown
July 30 Dramatic explosion of mine at Petersburg turns into the Battle of the Crater
August 18–25 Battles of the Weldon Railroad and Reams' Station
August 23 Lincoln submits to his cabinet a sealed memo stating that "it seems exceedingly probable that this Administration will not be re-elected," and pledging support after the election to the

president-elect
September 14–17 The Beefsteak Raid
September 19 Third Battle of Winchester
September 22 Battle of Fisher's Hill
September 29–October 7 Fighting around Richmond and Petersburg at Fort Harrison, Chaffin's Bluff, New Market Heights, Darbytown Road, and Boydton Plank Road
October 9 Cavalry fight at Tom's Brook
October 19 Battle of Cedar Creek
October 27 Battle of Burgess' Mill
November 8 President Lincoln re-elected with 55 percent of popular vote

1865 **February 5–7** Battle of Hatcher's Run
February 6 Lee appointed Commander-in-Chief of all Confederate armies by Congress, against President Davis's wishes—far too late to affect the prosecution of the war
March 2 Early's last remnant destroyed at the Battle of Waynesboro
March 4 Lincoln's Second Inaugural Address, "With malice toward none ..."
March 13 Confederate Congress approves raising of black troops
March 25 Attack on Fort Stedman near Petersburg
March 29–31 The final campaign in Virginia begins with fighting around Dinwiddie Court House
April 1 Battle of Five Forks
April 2 Confederate government evacuates Richmond
April 9 Lee surrenders to Grant at Appomattox Court House
April 14 Lincoln assassinated at Ford's Theater in Washington

1866 **April 2** State governments having been installed to meet Unionist directives, President Andrew Johnson officially proclaims "that the insurrection ... is at an end and is henceforth to be so regarded"

1877 The last enforced military government in the ex-Confederate states is removed, and home rule is restored at the state level

From innocents to warriors

No American war, and few of any other sort, has ever been fought with a lower proportion of trained soldiers than the American Civil War. The United States had from its origins suffered from a deep mistrust of standing armies and professional military men. The nation also wallowed in a nostalgic, but misguided, fondness for the notion of an untrained but devoted citizen-militia. At the outbreak of war in 1861, the United States Army included fewer than 15,000 officers and men; a few months later there would be more than one hundred times that many men under arms—far too many troops for the regular army to serve as an effective cadre.

A computerized index of official service records of both the Union and Confederate armies, completed in the year 2000, has for the first time made available hard data about the number of men mustered into service during the war. This is a subject about which arguments have raged among partisans of each side, and of various states, since the war years without any means of clear resolution. We now know that 1,231,006 Confederate service records exist, and 2,918,862 Federal records. Virginia supplied the largest Confederate increment, followed by Georgia and Tennessee. New York (456,720) led Federal recruitment, followed by Pennsylvania and Ohio. Those three Northern states, in fact, among them supplied almost as many troops as the entire Confederacy could muster. It should be recognized that the number of records does not indicate a precise number of men. Some Northern troops re-enlisted in different units at the expiration of a term of enlistment, and many Southern soldiers changed organizations in the spring of 1862 under the working of the new conscription law. Even so, the newly established totals of

service records constitute the first unmistakable benchmark on the subject.

Civil War soldiers almost without exception had been civilians in 1860. The census that year revealed the overwhelming advantages the Union enjoyed in numbers. The seceded states had a population of 9.1 million, 5.4 million of them white and therefore directly available for military

Confederate volunteers head off for war in 1861. (Public domain)

service. The other states counted 22.3 million inhabitants, and more than 800,000 alien passengers arrived at Northern ports during the war. The agrarian Confederacy faced even greater challenges in materiel. The 1860 census showed the South with only 7 percent of the nation's industrial output, 8 percent of its shipping, and one-fourth of its railroad mileage.

The capacities of the warring sides, described in detail in *The Civil War: Bull Run and Other Eastern Battles 1861–May 1863*, had begun by 1863 to play a steadily more important role in the progress of the conflict. The United States navy held unmistakable sway over all navigable waters, without any notable opposition. As a result, the portion of the Virginia Theater viable for Confederate operations extended no farther east than the fall lines of the several rivers flowing nominally eastward through the state: the Potomac, the Rappahannock, the James, and the Appomattox. Federal weaponry outmatched Southern equipment in every way. Union infantry carried rifles almost exclusively, while a substantial proportion of Confederates still had to make do with smoothbores (with one-tenth the range). As the conflict wore on, Northern cavalry would enjoy the advantage of breech-loading carbines, and eventually of repeating weapons. Union artillery fired farther and more accurately than Southern cannon, and Northern ordnance usually exploded on cue, whereas a Confederate battalion commander at Chancellorsville reported that only one in every 15 of his shells detonated.

By the spring of 1863, the organization and command of the main armies of the Virginia Theater had taken on distinctive characteristics. The Union Army of the Potomac had been tempered into a strong, resolute, military implement, patient in the face of steadily inept leadership. If President Abraham Lincoln would ever place a capable commander over the army, and support him, the veteran organization stood ready to be the bulwark of the national cause. The Confederate Army of Northern Virginia had long enjoyed superb direction from Lee, but without Stonewall Jackson to execute Lee's daring initiatives, a new mode of fighting would now be necessary.

As the contending armies in the Virginia Theater moved north in the late spring of 1863, away from Chancellorsville, they were pursuing a long and tortuous road that would lead them eventually to Gettysburg. They also were launching a new phase of the American Civil War.

Tredegar Iron Works in Richmond provided invaluable war materials, but the Confederacy had relatively few such industrial facilities. (Public domain)

The war without Jackson to Lee's last stand

The spring of 1863

A great, mournful cry went up all across the Confederacy as news spread in May 1863 of the death of General Thomas J. "Stonewall" Jackson, of wounds received at the Battle of Chancellorsville. A Georgia Confederate wrote dolefully on May 15 that "all hopes of Peace and Independence have forever vanished." Another Confederate told his wife back in Alabama, with more earnestness than literary precision: "Stonewall Jackson was kild ... I think this will have a gradeal to due with this war. I think the north will whip us soon." General Robert E. Lee faced the daunting task of reorganizing his army in Jackson's absence, and filling it with a sturdy spirit that could keep the "whip us soon" forecast from becoming a self-fulfilling prophecy.

Lee's stunning victory at Chancellorsville on May 1–6, against daunting odds, had generated enough momentum to carry the Confederate Army of Northern Virginia northward on a new campaign. (For Chancellorsville, see Gallagher, *The Civil War*.) Before he could launch such an effort, though, Lee had to reorganize his army to fill the yawning chasm left by Jackson's demise. He decided to go from the two-corps system that had worked so long and well for managing his infantry to an organization in three corps. The veteran General James Longstreet, reliable if contentious, kept command of the First Corps. General Richard S. Ewell, returning after nine months of convalescing from a wound, assumed command in late May of Jackson's old Second Corps. General A. P. Hill won promotion to command a new Third Corps composed of pieces extracted from the other two, combined with a few new units drawn to Virginia from service elsewhere in the Confederacy. General J. E. B. Stuart remained in command of the army's capable cavalry arm. Lee's artillery benefited from an excellent new organization into battalions, and from an officer corps that included many brilliant young men; but at the same time it suffered from inferior weaponry and at times from woefully inadequate ammunition.

Across the lines, General Joseph Hooker's Army of the Potomac loomed in Lee's way. The seasoned Northerners in that army by now knew their business thoroughly well and stood ready to continue their role as bulwark of the Federal Union. What they wanted and needed was a competent commander. At Chancellorsville, Hooker had demonstrated beyond serious contention that he was not such a man. The Army of the Potomac would finally receive a leader who matched its mettle in late June, but as the 1863 campaign unfolded, Hooker's palsied hand remained at the helm. His veteran corps commanders offered reliable leadership at the next level below Hooker.

After two consecutive battles along the line of the Rappahannock River, both armies knew the countryside intimately. Lee had won both battles in resounding fashion, but had not been able to exploit the victories into overwhelming triumphs that destroyed his enemy. Now he proposed to move north across the Potomac and carry the war into the enemy's country. Political hyperbole always insisted that the Confederates hoped to conquer the North and subjugate that much larger portion of the continent to some sort of serfdom. Such rodomontade, of course, reflected nothing of actual Southern aims.

Lee's move north must be recognized as a raid, not an invasion designed to conquer Pennsylvania or any other territory. He sought

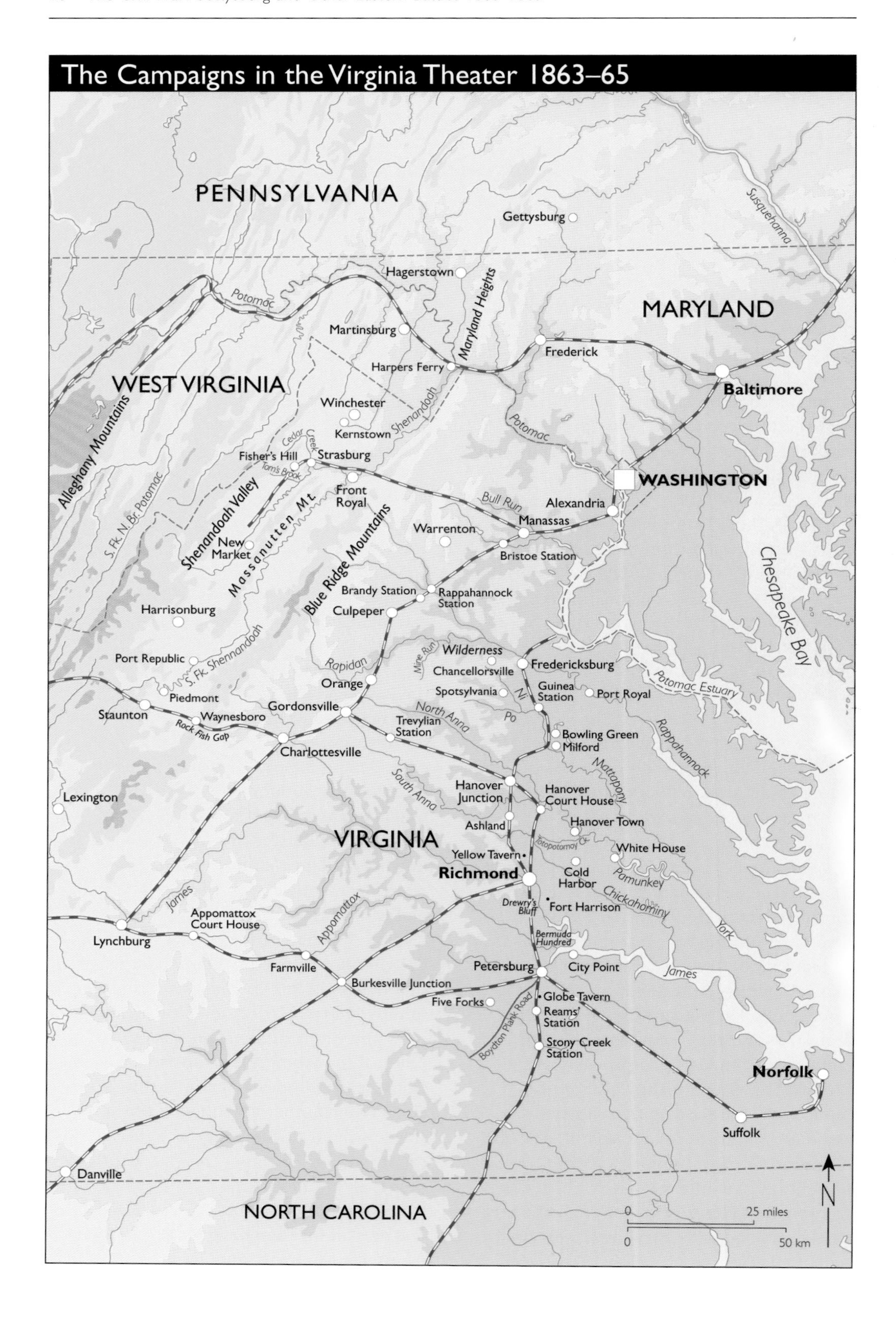
The Campaigns in the Virginia Theater 1863–65
PENNSYLVANIA
Gettysburg
Susquehanna
Hagerstown
Maryland Heights
MARYLAND
Potomac
Martinsburg
Frederick
Harpers Ferry
Baltimore
WEST VIRGINIA
Alleghany Mountains
Winchester
Kernstown
Shenandoah
Potomac
Cedar Creek
Fisher's Hill
Strasburg
Tom's Brook
WASHINGTON
S. Fk. N. Br. Potomac
Shenandoah Valley
Massanutten Mt.
Front Royal
Bull Run
Alexandria
Manassas
Blue Ridge Mountains
Warrenton
New Market
Bristoe Station
Chesapeake Bay
Brandy Station
Rappahannock Station
Harrisonburg
Culpeper
Mine Run
Wilderness
Port Republic
S. Fk. Shennandoah
Rapidan
Chancellorsville
Fredericksburg
Orange
Spotsylvania
Ni
Guinea Station
Port Royal
Potomac Estuary
Piedmont
North Anna
Staunton
Gordonsville
Po
Waynesboro
Rock Fish Gap
Trevylian Station
Rappahannock
Bowling Green
Milford
Charlottesville
Mattapony
South Anna
Hanover Junction
Hanover Court House
Lexington
Hanover Town
Ashland
VIRGINIA
Totopotomoy Ck
White House
Yellow Tavern
Cold Harbor
Richmond
Pamunkey
Chickahominy
Drewry's Bluff
Fort Harrison
James
Appomattox Court House
Appomattox
York
Bermuda Hundred
Lynchburg
City Point
Petersburg
James
Farmville
Burkesville Junction
Globe Tavern
Five Forks
Reams' Station
Boydton Plank Road
Stony Creek Station
Norfolk
Suffolk
Danville
N
NORTH CAROLINA
0
25 miles
0
50 km

The Confederates counterattack at Brandy Station. (Painting by Don Troiani, www.historicalartprints.com)

to lift the heel of war from Virginia, not only for humanitarian reasons, but also to allow that home country to recover from hostile occupation so that it could sustain Lee's army in future months. The country north of the Potomac also offered a much wider field for maneuver, a military element in which Lee excelled. An ostensible threat to the Federal political capital in Washington also held out potential advantages: knowing that his enemy *must* keep the city covered foreshadowed in mirror image the 1864 campaign in which Richmond served as a similar focus and pivot for Lee on the defensive.

The Confederate high tide at Chancellorsville propelled Lee's army into a new campaign that swept north past Winchester into Maryland and then Pennsylvania, where the Federal Army of the Potomac repulsed it in the war's largest battle. During the fall of 1863, the two armies clashed again in Virginia at Bristoe Station, Rappahannock Station, and Mine Run, but none of those engagements developed into a major battle. The next spring, with Commander-in-Chief U. S. Grant accompanying it, the Army of the Potomac crossed the Rapidan River and fought at Wilderness and Spotsylvania. Although they could not defeat Lee, the Federals determinedly pushed on to the North Anna River, Cold Harbor, and the outskirts of Richmond and Petersburg. After 10 months attempting to break into the Confederate capital, Grant finally succeeded in April 1865 and Lee was forced to surrender at Appomattox Court House on the 9th.

Lee moved away from Fredericksburg and the Rappahannock River line early in June 1863, and headed northwestward through piedmont Virginia toward the Shenandoah Valley. On June 9 his cavalry force fought one of the largest all-mounted engagements of the war around Brandy Station. Hooker had sent his own cavalry out with orders to "disperse and destroy" the Confederates they found, and the Northern troopers came close to doing that. They completely surprised the

General Joseph Hooker. (Public domain)

usually vigilant Southern mounted men early in the morning and drove them some distance. A rally on the low, rounded eminence of Fleetwood Hill saved the day for General Stuart's men. They inflicted about 1,000 casualties on the Northern attackers and suffered half that many themselves.

Brandy Station ended as a tactical draw, but Union troopers who had been battered relentlessly for two years had finally stood up to their adversaries and now had a positive experience upon which to build.

General J. E. B. ("Jeb") Stuart led most of the Confederate cavalry on a long ride around the Federal army en route to Pennsylvania, thus depriving Lee of his "eyes and ears" as he maneuvered toward Gettysburg. (Public domain)

The Battle of Gettysburg

"Jeb" Stuart's Southern cavalry again occupied center stage as the armies sidled northward and crossed the Potomac—or, more accurately, Stuart's cavalry exited stage right and became conspicuous by their absence. While Lee pushed north, into and through the Shenandoah Valley, Stuart embraced the chance to ride a raid entirely around the Union army. He had done just that twice before, in June and October 1862. This time the dashing maneuver backfired in deadly fashion. The cavalry detachment accompanying the main force in Stuart's absence had neither the men nor the leadership necessary to perform the essential function of screening Lee from enemy view, while simultaneously finding the enemy and tracking his progress and intentions. When Stuart finally rejoined Lee very tardily at Gettysburg, the commanding general said quietly, but in clear rebuke, "Well ... you are here at last," and "I had hoped to see you before this." Stuart's ride became one of the most-disputed subjects among postwar

Above. General George Gordon Meade took command of the Federal Army of the Potomac scant hours before the Battle of Gettysburg, but still won a great victory there. He has never received the credit he deserves for his achievement, largely because he scorned journalists and belonged to the wrong political party. (Public domain)

Left. Confederate General James Longstreet's behavior on July 2 remains the most controversial aspect of the Battle of Gettysburg. (Public domain)

Right. The war's largest battle engulfed the farms and hillsides around Gettysburg, Pennsylvania, on the first three days of July 1863. The Confederate army won a tremendous victory northwest of town on July 1 and swept through the streets in triumph. The Federals made a stand on a fishhook-shaped line south of Gettysburg, taking advantage of the slopes of Cemetery Ridge and anchored on the formidable heights of Culp's Hill and Little Round Top. Lee's efforts against the Federal right on July 2–3 met with very little success, but near the Round Tops the Confederates came close to a major success. On July 3, with his options dwindling, and loath to return to Virginia, Lee flung his center across open fields toward Cemetery Ridge. This attack, usually known as "Pickett's Charge," unfolded with immense drama and elicited tremendous courage from its participants, but yielded nothing for Lee but daunting casualties. He now had no choice but to retreat south toward Virginia.

The Battle of Gettysburg, July 1–3, 1863

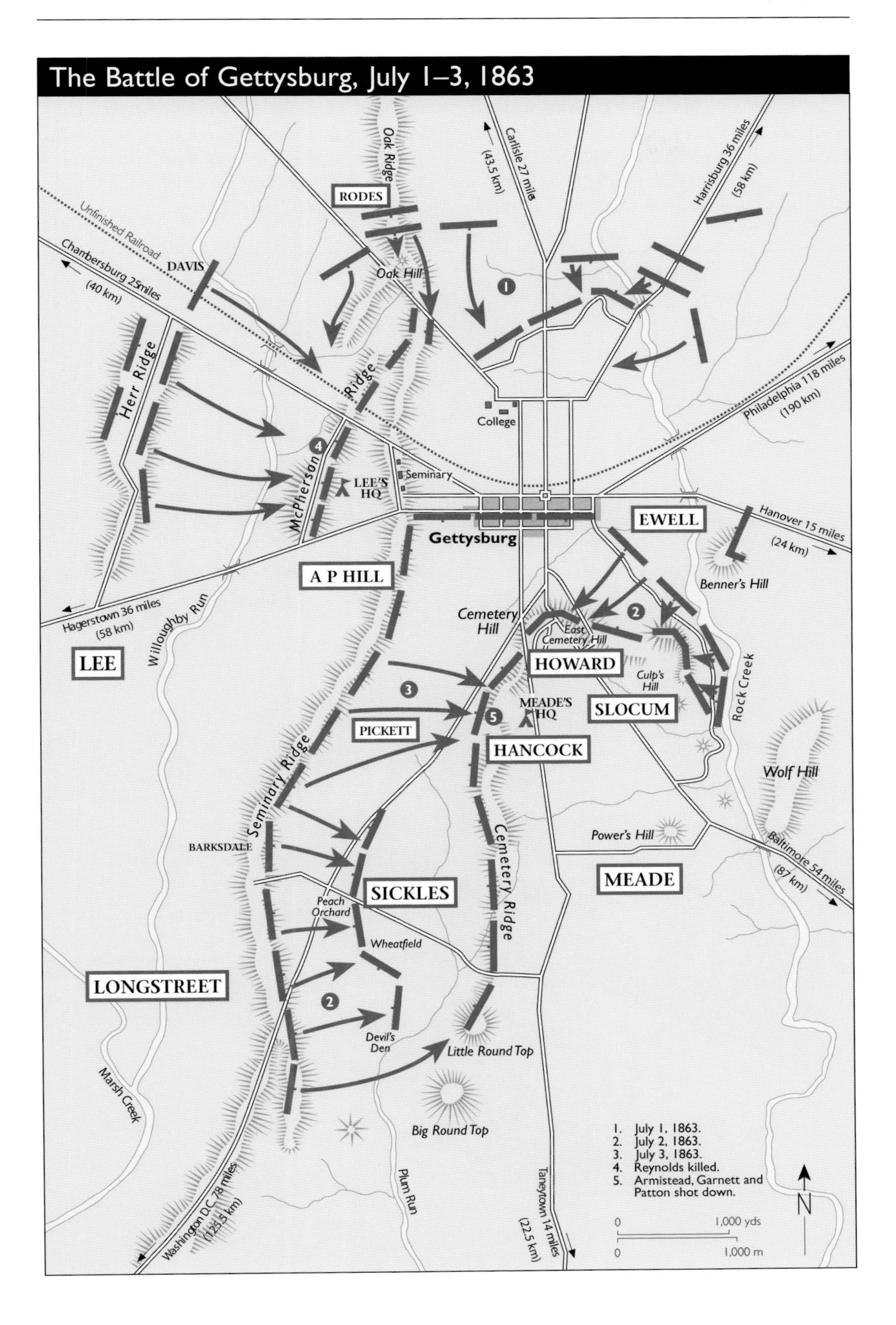

Confederates, and remains controversial to this day.

While Stuart galloped fecklessly across northern Virginia and Maryland and Pennsylvania, Lee's infantry achieved notable success at Winchester, Virginia, on June 14–15. Ewell's energy and success there prompted Southerners to hope that he would emerge as a sort of reincarnation of Stonewall Jackson. On through Maryland and deep into Pennsylvania the Confederate columns pressed. Some of them reached Carlisle and York and the outskirts of the state's capital city, Harrisburg. Fighting

at the crossroads town of Gettysburg that began on July 1 would draw all of them back south into the maw of the war's greatest battle. The long columns of blue-clad Union troops marching north through an arc surrounding Washington also wound up adjusting their route of march for that place. Gettysburg was a "meeting engagement" in every sense. No one picked the battle site. Roads drew small contending

A nineteenth-century view looking northwest from the crest of Little Round Top across the scenes of the heaviest fighting in the history of North America. (Public domain)

formations together and soon everyone else pitched in.

The battle of July 1, 1863, considered alone, must be adjudged one of the Army of Northern Virginia's greatest victories. Fighting opened that morning west of Gettysburg, a farming community of about 2,400 souls. Confederate skirmishers ran into Northern cavalry commanded by salty, unflappable General John Buford. A brigade of Southern infantry under President Jefferson Davis's nephew, General Joseph Davis, drove forward with marked success, but then the green brigadier clumsily allowed his men to be

Confederate General Lewis A. Armistead leads the desperate "Pickett's Charge" at the forefront, just before being mortally wounded. (Painting by Don Troiani, www.historicalartprints.com)

trapped in a deep cut of an unfinished railroad and lost most of them.

Confederate fortunes were abetted when a bullet killed Union General John F. Reynolds, a soldierly and much-admired officer commanding everything Federal on the field at that early hour. They benefited even more from the superb timing—the result of luck, not prescience—with which the fresh Southern division of General Robert E. Rodes dropped squarely onto the north flank of the Federal position. Intense fighting ensued on both sides of the road leading from Chambersburg to Gettysburg, with success perching first upon one banner then another, but the arrival of Rodes's division and other associated troops at a fortuitous point doomed Federal resistance. Eventually the whole Union line west of town collapsed and the Confederates enjoyed a field day chasing their fleeing foe into Gettysburg. Alexander Schimmelfennig, a Prussian-born general, eluded capture by hiding in a pigsty. Thousands of other men in blue became prisoners of war.

One of the battle's most-discussed turning points came as Confederates converged on Gettysburg from the north and west, and contemplated riding the crest of the tidal wave of momentum they had created. Lee characteristically left to the discretion of his new corps commander, General Ewell, the responsibility for continuing the advance. Possession of the crest of a long ridge that curled around Gettysburg and ran east to East Cemetery Hill and Culp's Hill would guarantee control of the military terrain for a considerable distance. Ewell equivocated, consulted, temporized—and never attacked. For the next two days, his troops would suffer mightily against the same two hills, by then strongly occupied, attacking again and again where he had not chosen to fight under far better terms. On the evening of July 1, Ewell did nothing. His inaction remains highly controversial today. The counter-factual question, "What would Jackson have done had he been there?" is, of course, unanswerable. A North Carolina soldier who fought there thought he knew. "We missed the genius of Jackson," he wrote a few days later. "The simplest soldier in the ranks felt it."

Federals scrambling to get to Gettysburg to blunt Lee's burgeoning success faced far better prospects than they would have a few days earlier. A Federal turning point in the campaign, indeed in the entire war in Virginia, had come on June 27 when General Hooker submitted his resignation in a fit of pique over having his wishes ignored. President Lincoln delightedly accepted the resignation and on June 28 General George Gordon Meade reluctantly took command of the Army of the Potomac.

Three days later Meade was fighting the war's largest battle. No American officer, in any war or era, has ever had so much crucial responsibility thrust upon him with such short notice. Meade met the challenge masterfully, beyond any imaginable degree that could have been expected, and far more ably than Hooker could have done. He confronted Lee's army at the high tide of Southern success, positioned deep in Federal country, and with Confederate numerical strength at a peak. At Gettysburg, Meade reached the battlefield as Lee swept everything before him late on July 1. Against those odds the brand-new Federal commander won a pivotal battle.

As a member of the US Congress before the war, Daniel E. Sickles had murdered his wife's lover and got away with the crime. At Gettysburg, he aggressively advanced his division on July 2 and became the target of a savage Confederate attack. (Public domain)

Meade's challenge early on July 2 was to restore confidence in his army and place it carefully on the powerful position available to him. The Federal line around Gettysburg resembled a fishhook. The shank of the fishhook ran straight south from town along Cemetery Ridge and ended on the massive anchor of two commanding hills, Big Round Top and Little Round Top. The hook curled around Gettysburg, turning east to another superb anchor at Culp's Hill. Meade's line enjoyed the obvious tactical advantage of high ground. Its hook also ensured the ability to exploit interior lines, with the invaluable privilege of reinforcing from one point to another directly and under cover. The sole tactical defect of the line was its vulnerability to artillery rounds pouring in from across a wide arc—the "converging fire" that is an artillerist's ideal. That defect never came into play. Confederate artillery, out-gunned and tacitly commanded by an ineffectual preacher-general, never levied converging fire against Meade's fishhook.

Although the great Confederate charge of July 3 garners the most attention, Gettysburg came to its decisive juncture on July 2 as Lee tried to exploit the advantages gained on the 1st. Meade resisted stoutly and to good effect, aided to some degree by Confederate failings. On the Federal right, Southern assaults against Culp's Hill faltered after much desperate bravery on both sides. The attack never came close to substantial success. At dusk, two brigades of Rebels pressed determinedly up the steep face of East Cemetery Hill—precisely where Ewell had feared to go the previous day under far more advantageous circumstances. Despite canister flung into their flanks, and Federal musketry in front, the Confederates reached the crest and held there for some time before Northern reinforcements flocked to the site in enough numbers to expel them. Meanwhile, the most portentous Confederate initiative during the Battle of Gettysburg had faltered far down on the Federal left, near the Round Tops.

At Chancellorsville, Lee had won a great victory by deploying to the point of decision a flanking column led by his most trusted subordinate, Stonewall Jackson. With Jackson dead, James Longstreet was clearly Lee's primary military asset. Longstreet did not want to fight on the offensive, however, and apparently spent July 1–3 sulking over Lee's variant view of things. Such defensive triumphs as the Battle of Fredericksburg appealed to Longstreet (and every other Confederate), but how often would one find a pliant Ambrose Burnside willing to slaughter his own army? Longstreet did not wish to take the initiative at all, so only grudgingly—and very tardily—moved away with Lee's maneuver element. The army commander remained near his other corps commanders, both of them brand new. After a sluggish march, marked by confusion and backtracking, Longstreet's column arrived opposite the Federal left in front of the two Round Tops.

The nature of the violent combat that swept across the fields and hills south of Gettysburg on July 2 was affected in a fundamental way by the impulsive actions of Federal General Daniel E. Sickles. The General came not from a military background but from the political realm, having been a powerful Congressman from New York. Sickles' legacy includes not just his Civil War service, but also a series of bumptious endeavors: he killed his wife's lover before the war, and escaped on a plea of temporary insanity; as postwar US ambassador to Spain, he had an affair with that country's queen; and he played the central role in preserving Gettysburg battlefield early in the twentieth century. In July 1863, Sickles always insisted, he had saved the battle itself for the Union, by pushing forward in front of the main line

General George E. Pickett, a foppish fellow of starkly limited capacity, became one of the most famous names in American military history because of the mighty charge on July 3, 1863. He and his division did little else during the war. (Public domain)

without Meade's permission. As Longstreet slowly approached action, Sickles moved forward into his path.

The assault by Longstreet's Confederates drove Sickles off his new position, and cost the Federal general his leg (after the war, a Congressman once again, Sickles took visiting constituents to the medical museum in Washington to show them his leg bones, donated as an exhibit). General William Barksdale of Mississippi, as fiery an antebellum politician as Sickles had been, led a dramatic charge into Sickles' line. Southerners swept east and northeast in a wide arc that resulted in bitter fighting across a landscape that became forever famous: The Peach Orchard; The Wheatfield; Devil's Den; Little Round Top. The latter position held the key to that sector of the battlefield, looking down on the others and also commanding Cemetery Ridge to the north. After a desperate struggle, Confederates from Texas and Alabama receded from the crest of the hill, leaving a ghastly harvest of prostrate comrades behind them. As darkness fell, the Federals held the

Depiction of one segment of the fighting on July 3, from the immense 19th-century cyclorama painting by Philippoleaux, the largest piece of Gettysburg art and probably the most famous. (Ann Ronan Picture Library)

key ground and Lee's great opportunity had passed. Controversy still rages over the efficacy of Sickles' relocation, and about Longstreet's lassitude in moving to battle.

Impeccable hindsight shows convincingly that Lee's decision to attack the next day, July 3 , against Meade's center, was his worst of the war. He doubtless undertook the forlorn hope because it seemed the only remaining option he had to get at his enemy. The Army of Northern Virginia had

Confederate Colonel Waller T. Patton fell dreadfully wounded at the height of "Pickett's Charge." He died 18 days later as a prisoner of war.

reached the end of a very long supply limb, about 120 miles (190 km) from the nearest railroad-served depot back in the Shenandoah Valley. Stocks of commissary, quartermaster, and ordnance stores (particularly artillery ammunition) had dwindled and could not be renewed. Overwhelming tactical success on July 1 had yielded the opportunity for an even greater triumph on July 2, but that opportunity dissolved under frustrating circumstances. Lee's infantry had never failed to do what he asked of them. Might not a full fresh division of them, just arrived on the field, with support from other units and massed artillery, break the Federal center?

In the event, they could not. About 12,000 Confederates tried, in the most renowned attack in all of American military history. "Pickett's Charge" actually included about as many men from other units as from General George E. Pickett's division, which prompted postwar quarrels about the event's famous name. Confederate Colonel E. Porter Alexander massed artillery for a thunderous advance barrage, which used up much of the tenuous supply of shells. The barrage also fired too high against a target obscured by smoke and dust. When the infantry stepped out, they faced a maelstrom of shell-fire, then canister at closer range, and finally musketry in sheets as they charged past the humble farmhouse of the Codori family. A Virginian in Pickett's command wrote: "On swept the column over ground covered with dead and dying men, where the earth seemed to be on fire, the smoke dense and suffocating, the sun shut out, flames blazing on every side, friend could hardly be distinguished from foe."

Generals Lewis A. Armistead and Richard B. Garnett suffered mortal wounds at the front of the attack. Garnett's body was never recovered from the carnage, although his sword turned up in a pawn shop years later. Fully one-half of their men went down as well (Northern losses reached perhaps 1,500). A handful of brave Confederates broke into the Federal line for a time and hand-to-hand fighting raged around a battery near an angle in a stone fence. A Northern major marveled at how "the rebels ... stood there, against the fence, until they were nearly all shot down." They had reached what often has been called "the high-water mark of the Confederacy."

When the survivors turned back in sullen retreat, they suffered as dreadfully as on the way in. Among the Southern officers mangled was Colonel Waller Tazewell Patton, one of six brothers in the army and a great-uncle of the General Patton famous during the Second World War. The Colonel had grasped a cousin's hand, said "it is our turn next," and leaped over the stone wall at the attack's high-water mark, then went down with his lower jaw shot away. As he lay dying in a Federal hospital, unable to talk, "Taz" scribbled a note to his mother: "my only regret is that there are no more brothers left to defend our country."

Fighting continued on July 3 in lesser volume on the far Federal right at Culp's Hill, and Jeb Stuart's cavalry engaged mounted foe well behind the main Union line, but Pickett's Charge proved to be the final major engagement of the Battle of Gettysburg. Each army had lost about 25,000 men. During the night of July 4–5, Lee's army began to retreat toward the Potomac River through a violent rainstorm. The miles-long column of wagons bearing suffering and dying men became a train of utter misery. Meade pursued with some energy. Skirmishing flared along the route each day, but by July 14 Lee had managed to cross the rain-swollen river back into Virginia across a set of precarious pontoon bridges.

General Meade came in for more calumny than praise. President Lincoln was disgusted that he had not captured the entire Confederate force, which looked far easier on a Washington map than on a muddy Maryland ridgeline. George Meade had won the war's largest battle, scant hours after taking command, and had done so against an enemy army that had been inevitably triumphant theretofore; but politicians and press, followed eventually by many historical writers, grumbled that he should have done more.

Meade commanded the Army of the Potomac for the rest of the war as by far its most successful leader. In a very real sense, he saved the Union—yet he has never received much recognition for his achievement. That is probably because General U. S. Grant subsequently came east at a convenient moment, when numbers and materiel made it possible simply to wage a war of attrition against the Confederacy.

The fall and winter of 1863–64

The perspective of years seems to suggest that Gettysburg turned the war onto a new axis, especially when taken with Federal conquest of the Mississippi river through the fall of Vicksburg on July 4. History is, of course, lived forward but written backward. Americans struggling to further their opposite causes in 1863 saw little of what is now said to have been obvious. Confederates who fought at Gettysburg, and their families writing from home, rued the reverse they had suffered, but almost never displayed any notion of impending doom. When the Yankees came back across the Potomac, they believed, the invaders would be as susceptible to defeat as they always had been—and the veteran Confederate army set about to prove it.

Back on Virginian soil, Lee resumed his adroit maneuvering to counter each Unionist initiative, and proved to be almost uniformly successful in foiling his enemy. The armies edged southward and eastward, out of the Shenandoah Valley and into piedmont country, finally fetching up about 40 miles (64 km) of latitude south of the Potomac. Through the late summer and fall of 1863, operations centered on a corridor between Warrenton and Culpeper and Orange. None of the sallies and probes evolved into a major engagement. Lee dispatched Longstreet in early September with one-third of the army's infantry to the Western Theater, where the reinforcements would arrive just in time to play a crucial role in the Battle of Chickamauga. Two

General Ambrose Powell Hill had been one of Lee's most capable division leaders, but at Bristoe Station and elsewhere he failed to perform up to his commander's expectations. (Public domain)

Federal corps followed Longstreet west, where they spent the rest of the war. Longstreet returned to Virginia in the following spring.

Lee's reduced strength threw him squarely on the defensive. Meade promptly pushed his foe south of the Rapidan River in mid-September, but on October 9 Lee grasped the initiative again, as he so much preferred to do. The Confederates advanced columns around both of Meade's flanks, forcing the Federal army to fall back north beyond Warrenton toward Manassas. A. P. Hill's troops took the lead. Hill had been almost invisible at Gettysburg during his first battle at the helm of the Third Corps. Now he had the advance at a portentous moment on October 14.

Unfortunately, Hill displayed more dash than judgment. Without reconnoitering the position, he threw two brigades of North Carolinians at a Union force ensconced behind a railroad embankment at Bristoe Station. The Northerners proved to be the entire Federal II Corps, veteran and unmovable. The Carolinians fell in windrows without any hope of success, losing about 1,400 men in a short interval. The Federal II Corps then withdrew unmolested. Lee conveyed his sad reaction to Hill in a typically restrained rebuke. As the two generals rode across the scene and Hill sought to explain how the disaster unfolded, Lee said quietly: "Well, well, General, bury these poor men and let us say no more about it."

Three weeks after Bristoe Station, the Federals inflicted another minor disaster on Lee's army. Confederates in Virginia were accustomed to achieving most of their goals, and had never been driven from a fixed, well-defended position. When Lee fell back across the Rappahannock River in the aftermath of Bristoe Station, he incautiously left a *tête-de-pont* on the river's north bank at Rappahannock Station. A reliable brigade of Louisiana infantry occupied strong entrenchments north of the river, and artillery posted on the south bank offered supporting fire. When General Jubal A. Early, commanding the Confederates in the vicinity, noticed enemy strength concentrating nearby, he sent another brigade of infantry across to support the Louisianians.

Both brigades were doomed. Union General John Sedgwick closed in on the position with his VI Corps on November 7, 1864. A bright young West Point graduate (he had just turned 24), Colonel Emory Upton, led the advance with determination and swept over the works. Outflanked Confederates raced for safety across the pontoon bridges that connected the bridgehead with the southern bank. Only by means of a daring exploit were the Southerners able to cut loose the pontoon bridges and put the river between themselves and the victorious enemy. The Federals had inflicted about 2,000 casualties, most of them in the form of prisoners. The youthful Upton would be heard from again with another daring attack the following May, and then as a leader in reorganizing the United States Army after the war.

The youthful Emory Upton had much to do with the striking Federal success at Rappahannock Station. He would be heard from again at Spotsylvania Court House and Cold Harbor, and after the war would play a central role in the reorganization of the United States Army. (Public domain)

With the Rappahannock line breached, Meade could move into the excellent bivouac country south of that river and north of the Rapidan. For the next six months, the Rapidan River would constitute the military frontier in Virginia. (The river

Modern aerial view of Wilderness Battlefield, looking east down the Orange Turnpike. The open space is Saunders Field, where the heaviest fighting raged on May 5–6, 1864. General Grant's headquarters were situated on the north *(left)* of the main road, where it bends left near the top of the photo.

had been named in colonial times for British Queen Anne. Its rapid flow prompted settlers to call the stream the "Rapid Anne," subsequently shortened to Rapidan.) Skirmishing through the fall of 1863 and the following winter only threatened major operations once, at the end of November. On the 26th, Confederates who had been easing into what they thought would be winter quarters learned that Meade was moving in strength toward crossings lower on the Rapidan, not far west of the familiar ground around Chancellorsville.

Elements of the contending armies collided on November 27 at Payne's Farm and a hot, confused fight blossomed. Much of it raged in densely wooded country. Captain John C. Johnson of the 50th Virginia, "a large and stout man of about fifty years of age," who towered over most of his men at 6'7" (2 m) of height, decided that his men "were not doing as well as they ought." To shame them into maintaining a steadier fire, Johnson stalked to the crest of the position, lay down on the ground, "broadside to the enemy," and told his men that "if they were afraid ... they could use him as a breastwork." Undaunted and pragmatic, several infantrymen did just that, resting their rifles on Johnson and firing "steadily from that position until the fight was over." Johnson survived the gesture, and also a chest wound he suffered in 1864 and two periods as a prisoner of war, to return home in 1865.

Once both sides had tested their opponents around Payne's Farm, the engagement there became the nexus upon which a long set of parallel lines spread across the countryside just south of the Rapidan. During the last three days of November and the first day of December, men in uniforms of both colors spent more time digging than shooting. A weather front brought in bitter cold and whistling wind on the heels of a long downpour, making everyone miserable at the same time that it reduced the potential for major military movements on the region's few and poor roads.

Meade's lines ran north–south, facing west toward Lee's position. Between the two ran Mine Run, which gave its name to the week-long action. Meade prepared a major turning movement around the Confederate right (southern) flank for the morning of November 30, but when the time came he recognized that his foe was ready to repulse the attack from strong works. The Pennsylvanian courageously cancelled the attack and two days later recrossed the Rapidan, having lost about 1,500 men south of the river. Lee and most of his soldiers were bitterly disappointed. "We should never have permitted those people to get away," Lee seethed.

Meade recognized that sending the vain assault forward would have been popular with President Lincoln and elsewhere in Washington, but he wrote officially, "I cannot be a party to a wanton slaughter of my troops for any mere personal end." To his wife, Meade admitted, "I would rather be ignominiously dismissed, and suffer anything, than knowingly and wilfully have thousands of brave men slaughtered for nothing." His estimate doubtless was correct: had he thrown in attacks that cost 10,000 (or even 15,000) more men, he surely would have enjoyed, and retain to this day, a glossier image. He might have retained independent control of the Army of the Potomac and emerged as the war's great hero in the North.

As the armies filed away from the Mine Run earthworks, they were ending a year of campaigning that had taken them on broad sweeps across Virginia, Maryland, and Pennsylvania. Only twice during 1863, however, had they fought full-scale, pitched engagements. Chancellorsville was the largest battle ever fought in Virginia, and Gettysburg the costliest of the entire war; but 1863 had produced far less intense combat than the armies had experienced in 1862. The soldiers who settled into winter camps in December 1863 faced, unawares, a new year that would bring far more fighting than the year just past, and under far different circumstances.

Into the Wilderness

In May 1864, the Federal army advanced across the Rapidan River and ended a period of six months during which that stream had, almost without interruption, constituted the military frontier between the United States and the Confederate States. General Robert E. Lee's Army of Northern Virginia had spent the winter spread across the rolling fields beyond the right bank of the river in Orange County, around Orange Court House and Gordonsville and Verdiersville. General George G. Meade's Federal Army of the Potomac wintered in the piedmont countryside north of the Rapidan, centered on Culpeper Court House.

Southern troops by this time had begun to suffer markedly for want of rations, both in volume and in quality, at least in part because the president of the key rail line in central Virginia was an antebellum immigrant from the North who secretly accepted pay from the Federal Secretary of War. Northern troops enjoyed infinitely better supplies. Their army also underwent a profound change during this winter. Meade remained its nominal commander, and would occupy that role to the war's end. The newly minted Commander-in-Chief of all Federal armies, however, established his headquarters next to Meade, leaving the army commander consigned to a secondary profile. Ulysses S. Grant had come east as the hero of benchmark Federal triumphs at Vicksburg and Chattanooga to be commissioned into the newly created rank of lieutenant-general. For the rest of the war, Meade's army commonly appeared in the press as "Grant's army" because the Commander-in-Chief was with it. Writing on the war still uses that locution, and in fact it will appear this way in most instances through the rest of this book.

As spring hardened the roads in 1864, "Grant's army" prepared to take the offensive with a new-found determination imparted by Grant himself. A reorganization consolidated some of the familiar old corps out of existence, leaving only the II, V, and VI Corps. General Ambrose E. Burnside's IX Corps also marched with the army. The once-disgraced Burnside had enough political currency to have landed back in corps command, and to be immune to Meade's orders. He would report directly to Grant, in awkward contravention of the most basic principles of unity of command.

The combined Federal force that crossed the Rapidan at the beginning of May numbered about 120,000 men. Lee could counter with only a few more than half as many troops, including Longstreet's infantry, newly returned from their adventures (and mis-adventures) in Tennessee and Georgia. Grant could—and did—draw on innumerable reinforcements through the coming campaign; the Confederate manpower cupboard by this time had become close to bare.

Grant intended to move south across the Rapidan east of Lee's army and slice straight through "the Wilderness" to get between his enemy and Richmond. That would force Lee to react rapidly under circumstances in which his enemy could choose the terms of engagement. Much late-twentieth-century writing has professed to recognize the striking wisdom that places did not matter, only the enemy's army. Lee and his government knew better. Richmond must be held for an array of fundamental reasons, industrial, logistical, military, political, and spiritual. When it in fact fell in April 1865, the war in Virginia ended almost concurrently. Grant's attempt to force Lee's small army to defend the approaches to Richmond in the spring of 1864 was precisely the right formula.

Getting through the Wilderness proved to be far more difficult than Grant had hoped. The dense second-growth thickets that gave the region its name covered about 70 square miles (180 km^2) on the south bank of the Rapidan–Rappahannock line, about 12 miles (19 km) wide and six miles (9.5 km) deep. When Lee received word that his adversary had crossed the Rapidan into the Wilderness, he hurled his troops eastward and they struck the Federal right flank like a

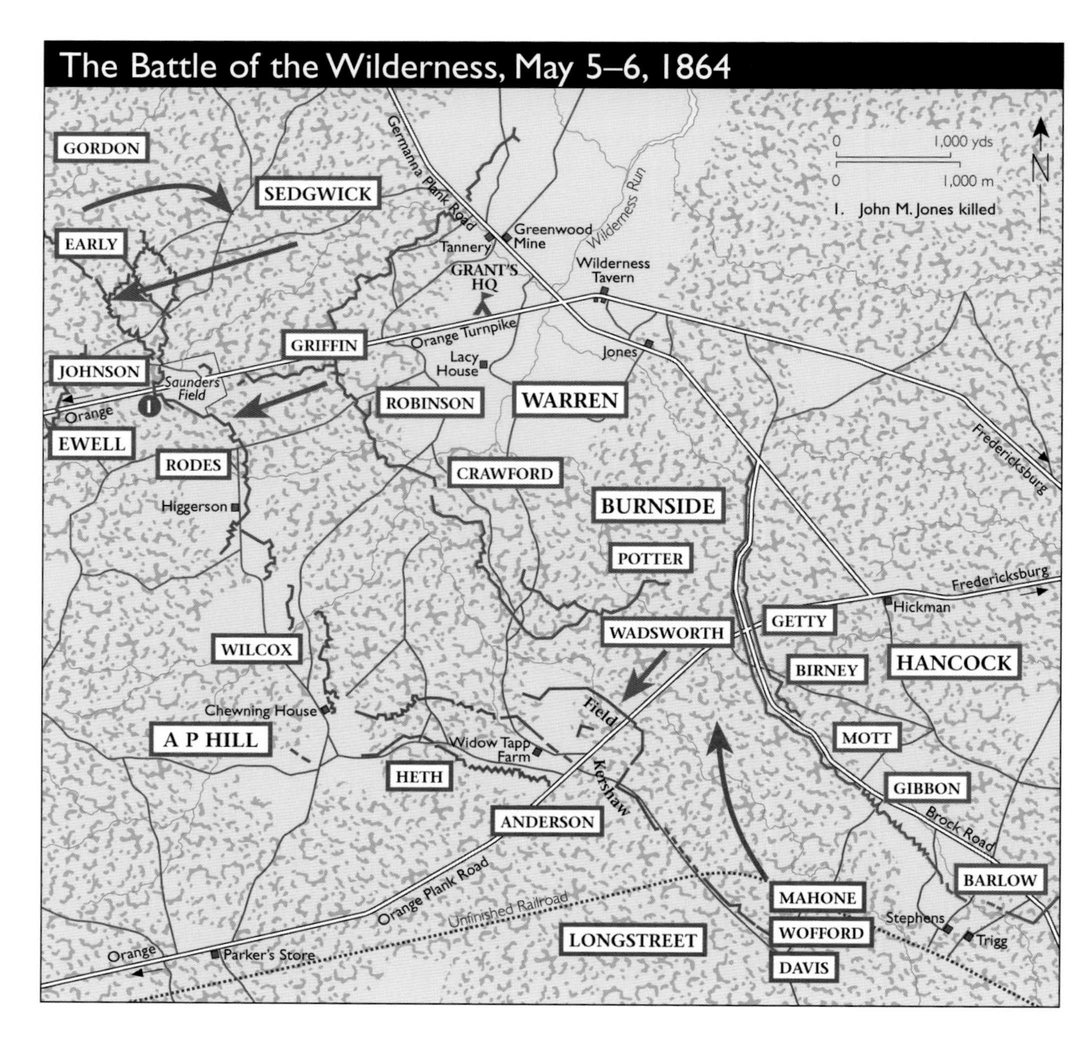

The first clash between the war's two most famous leaders, Robert E. Lee and U. S. Grant, unfolded in the dense thickets of "the Wilderness" on May 5–6, 1864. Grant's plan to slip across Lee's front and get between him and the Confederate capital at Richmond crumbled when the Confederates came in from the west and struck him a violent blow. For two days the fighting raged in woods and the few clearings, notably Saunders Field and the Widow Tapp Farm, and along the corridors of the Orange Turnpike and the Orange Plank Road. The Federals came close to success in each of the sectors, which were fought in virtual isolation from each other because of the underbrush; but on May 6 Confederate attacks turned and shattered both Federal flanks. On May 7, Grant moved southeast away from the Wilderness, toward Spotsylvania Court House.

thunderbolt. The Brock Road offered Grant and Meade the only practicable route southward through the Wilderness. Two east–west roads served Lee as corridors of advance and attack. The old Orange Turnpike ran 2.5 miles (4 km) north of the parallel Orange Plank Road. Densely scrubby country separated them. The intersections of the two Orange roads with the Brock Road network became the focus of the strivings of both armies for two days, May 5–6, 1864.

The Battle of the Wilderness erupted on the Orange Turnpike on the morning of the 5th when Federal detachments in that quarter saw Confederates of General Richard S. Ewell's corps threatening from the west. Grant directed Meade to attack. Meade sent General Gouverneur K. Warren's V Corps. The Confederates had begun to build earthworks along the crest of a ridge at the western edge of a 40-acre (16-ha) open space known locally as Saunders Field. When Warren's men marched in determined ranks into the field and started up the other side, they were inaugurating a pattern that defined much of the subsequent two days of fighting on the Turnpike. Confederate firepower pouring down the slope into Saunders Field, from behind defensive works, proved more than flesh and blood could stand—both at the first attack and through many others that followed. An early Unionist surge did attain the western crest, killing Southern General John M. Jones and breaking the line. However, Confederates pounding rapidly eastward on the Turnpike soon ejected the interlopers and restored the position.

Much of General John Sedgwick's Federal V Corps went to Warren's aid. Throughout May 5 men on both sides, particularly the blue-clad attackers, died in the struggle for Saunders Field. A section of guns stranded between the lines served as a magnet for repeated hand-to-hand strife. At day's end, the initial situation around the field remained unchanged despite a daunting expenditure of blood: Federals held the eastern edge, Confederates the western.

The thickets of the Wilderness, broken by only a few rude paths and desolate farmsteads, made maneuvering and fighting on a large scale impracticable between the Turnpike and the Plank Road. Both armies recognized the potential advantage of using the unoccupied middle ground as a means of threatening an exposed enemy rear; both made gestures toward exploiting the opportunity; neither ever managed to effect a serious lodgment.

Meanwhile, a separate battle raged on the Orange Plank Road, nearly in isolation from

The Texans turn Lee back on the Widow Tapp Farm, Wilderness Battlefield. (Painting by Don Troiani, www.historicalartprints.com)

events a few miles to the north. General A. P. Hill's Confederate Third Corps moved eastward on the Plank Road. The sturdy Federal II Corps, commanded by the indomitable General Winfield Scott Hancock, interposed an obstacle between Hill and the crucial intersection. General George W. Getty's division, extracted from VI Corps up on the Turnpike, hurried south to help Hancock hold the Brock–Plank crossroads. Bitter fighting seethed through the confusing thickets. Men died by the hundreds and fell maimed by the thousands.

Federal strength threatened to overwhelm Hill, but at the end of May 5 he had held. One-third of Lee's infantry, the First Corps under General James Longstreet, did not reach the battlefield at all on May 5 . Hill's troops, weary and decimated and ill-organized, lay in the brush of the Wilderness that night with the desolate awareness that they could not withstand a serious attack in the morning.

The arrival of Longstreet's first troops early on May 6 salvaged a desperate situation for Lee and resulted in a moment of high personal drama for the Southern leader. Hancock had carefully arranged for a broad attack on both sides of the Plank Road. Soon after dawn, he launched his assault with characteristic vigor. It rolled steadily forward, scattering Hill's regiments and threatening to rupture Lee's entire front. Artillery had been of little use in the thickets, but a battalion of a dozen Confederate guns lined the woods at the western edge of the Tapp field, a 30-acre (12.14 ha) clearing around the rude cabin and modest farm of a widow named Tapp—the only sizable open space anywhere in the battle zone along the Plank Road. The cannon flung canister across the Tapp Farm space in double-shotted doses, making the ground untenable for Union infantry. Northern troops filtered around the edge of the clearing to get in behind the guns and complete the victory. Then, without any time whatsoever to spare, the van of Longstreet's column reached the point of crisis.

Among the first units up was the famed Texas Brigade, perhaps Lee's best shock troops. The battles that had won the Texans their well-deserved renown had cost them enormous casualties: fewer than 800 of them remained to carry muskets into the Wilderness that morning. As the brigade moved resolutely through the hard-pressed artillery, Lee rode quietly beside them. The General recognized his army's peril, and had determined to take a personal role in repairing the rupture. When the Texans noticed him, and recognized his intention,

The final Confederate attack on May 6 swept all the way to the Brock Road, but could not hold the position. (Public domain)

"a yell rent the air that must have been heard for miles around." The Texans urged Lee to go back, shouting that they would not go forward until he did so. A soldier (there would later be dozens of claimants for the honor) grasped Lee's bridle and turned him back.

A participant in the event, writing soon thereafter, noted that Lee had not said much, but it was "his tone and look, which each one of us knew were born of the dangers of the hour" that "so infused and excited the men." A Texan next to the observer, "with tears coursing down his cheeks and yells issuing from his throat exclaimed, 'I would charge ... itself for that old man.'"

Lee went back. The Texans went forward and redeemed their pledge. Federal bullets hit nearly three-fourths of them within a few minutes, but they stabilized the situation and saved the day. The "Lee-to-the-Rear" episode immediately became an integral part of army lore. A monument at the spot today says simply, "Lee to the rear, cried the Texans, May 6, 1864."

Once Longstreet's reinforcements had stabilized the situation, the Confederate commanders looked for a means to regain the initiative. They found it in an unfinished

Hundreds of helpless wounded men of both sides burned to death when muzzle flashes lit the thickets of the Wilderness on fire. (Public domain)

railroad—graded and filled, but not yet tracked—that ran south of and parallel to the Plank Road. A mixed force of four brigades pulled from various divisions got astride the rail corridor, moved east until opposite the dangling Federal left flank, then turned north and completely routed Hancock's troops. In Hancock's words, the Confederates rolled up his line "like a wet blanket." Most of the attackers pushed as far north as the Plank Road. Some of them actually went into the woods north of the road.

In the ensuing chaos, a mistaken "friendly" volley tore into a cavalcade of Confederate officers reconnoitering on the road. It killed General Micah Jenkins and inflicted a dreadful wound on Longstreet. Lee's most capable surviving subordinate eventually recovered, but he would be out of service until long after the war had settled into a siege at Petersburg. The fatal volley, reminiscent of the mistaken fire that had mortally wounded Stonewall Jackson nearby exactly one year earlier, extracted all the energy from the Confederate success. An attack later in the day pressed all the way to the heart of the enemy line on the Brock Road, but in the end it produced nothing but more losses.

While Lee inspired the Texans and then regained the initiative on the Plank Road, General Ewell's Confederates continued to hold firm control of their crucial wood line up on the Turnpike. General John B. Gordon—a non-professional soldier who would bloom late in the conflict into a remarkable warrior—spent much of May 6 attempting to secure permission for an attack in the woods on the far left, where Grant had failed to protect his right flank. Timidity ruled Ewell's behavior by this time in the war (he had lost a leg and gained an extremely strong-willed wife, with deleterious impact upon his élan and *amour-propre*). By the time Gordon extracted authority to attack, daylight was dwindling. Even so, the surprise assault captured two Yankee generals and hundreds of men, and thoroughly shattered Grant's flank. In a ghastly aftermath to the Wilderness fighting, leaves and brush caught fire from muzzle flashes and hundreds of helpless wounded men of both sides burned to death.

For two weeks, Lee's Confederates stubbornly resisted the Federal army under Grant and Meade in the woods and fields around Spotsylvania Court House. After Confederates won the race for the key intersection on May 8, both armies entrenched on a steadily widening front. On May 10, a Federal assault broke into the Doles' salient and two days later about 25,000 Northern troops crushed the nose of the Mule Shoe. Lee hurriedly constructed a new final line across the base of the Mule Shoe, and easily repulsed an attack against the position on May 18. The next day, a brisk fight at the Harris Farm, northeast of the main battlefield, ended major action at Spotsylvania. On the 21st, Grant moved southeast in a new attempt to interpose between Lee and Richmond.

The Battle of Spotsylvania Court House

After two days of intense combat in the Wilderness, Grant had lost about 18,000 men, Lee perhaps 8,000 (Confederate casualties for the last year of the war are difficult to ascertain with any precision). Wilderness was the only major battle in the Virginia Theater in which an army had both of its flanks shattered. Grant had vivid, immediate proof that fighting Lee would be nothing at all like toying with Generals Bragg and Johnston and Pemberton in the west. Nothing daunted, the Federal Commander-in-Chief calmly determined

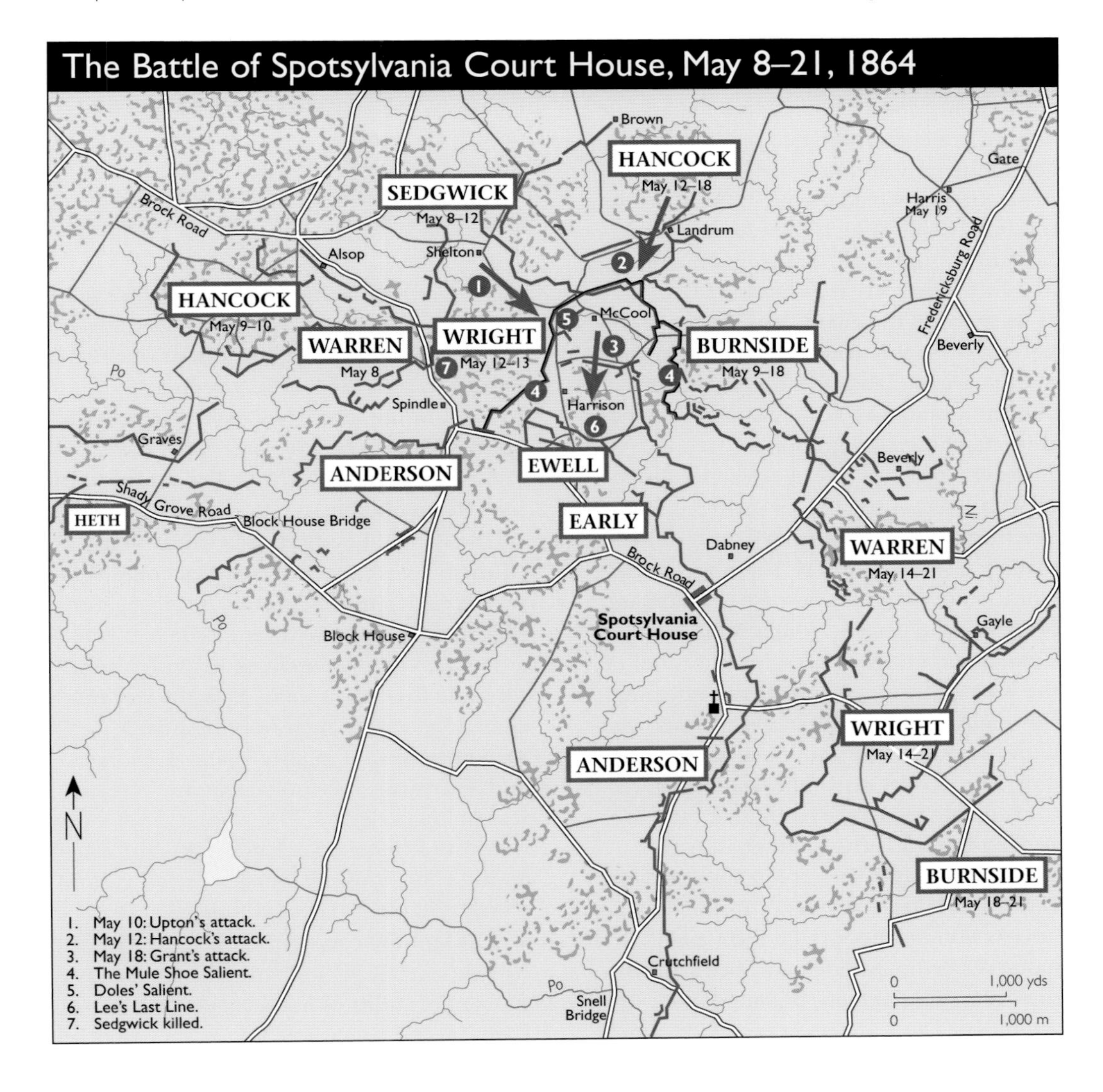

The Battle of Spotsylvania Court House, May 8–21, 1864

to press southward again, keeping the pressure on Lee.

Early on May 7, Grant issued orders to leave the Wilderness and head southeast toward Spotsylvania Court House, where the regional road net afforded a chance to slip between Lee and Richmond. When Grant turned south, despite having suffered as grievous losses as had prompted other commanders to return north, he put the war in Virginia onto a new track. Soldiers sensed the new resolve when they divined the direction of the move, and cheered boisterously. Tens of thousands of them would be shot in the next four weeks, but the army would continue to press steadily southward.

The march toward Spotsylvania Court House turned into a dramatic race fraught with mighty consequences. In a remarkable bout of prescience, Lee had ordered months before the improvement of a set of woods roads that paralleled the Brock Road, leading toward Spotsylvania. He selected General Richard H. Anderson, a phlegmatic officer, to replace temporarily the wounded Longstreet at the head of the First Corps. Anderson put his troops on the road to Spotsylvania, and found no good place to stop because of burning woods and narrow byways—so he kept marching all night long.

Federal progress on the far better Brock Road faltered in the face of scattered, but determined, resistance from Confederate cavalry. General Philip H. Sheridan, a Grant crony from the west, was new to command of the Federal cavalry, which should have shouldered the gray-clad skirmishers out of the way with ease. Sheridan was scheming this night, however, about getting out from under Meade's orders and instead reporting directly to his friend Grant. As a result, the Confederate resistance held on at one sketchy position after another all night.

Early on May 8 the race to Spotsylvania ended with Confederates controlling the key intersection on the Spindle Farm a matter of moments before Meade's advance arrived there. The consequence of Sheridan's indifference and Anderson's inability to stop

Confederates used felled trees covered with earth to fabricate an intricate set of field fortifications unlike anything that had been used earlier in the war. This view is in the vicinity of the nose of the Mule Shoe, near what became "the Bloody Angle." (Public domain)

was a very narrow margin of success for the Confederates. All day long, Federals trudged across an open field into Southern rifle fire, hoping to gain the intersection that they had lost in the race. They never succeeded, on May 8 or on several subsequent days. Thousands of them fell killed or wounded in the forlorn attempts.

The Battle of Spotsylvania Court House churned across a broad stretch of country for two weeks, from the meeting engagement on May 8 until May 21. Never before had field armies in Virginia remained in close contact for more than a few days. Now the war was changing, edging away from dash and maneuver toward mighty defensive works and, eventually, positional warfare resembling a siege.

Most of General Lee's defensive line at Spotsylvania took advantage of good ground along a ridge that covered four miles (6.4 km) of farming country between the Po and Ni rivers. From the point at which the May 8 race ended, units of both sides spread in both directions, entrenching as they went.

Federal reinforcements pressed southwest toward the Po, hoping to get beyond Lee's flank; Confederates arrived to counter them. When both armies' flanks reached the Po, Federals began to push in the opposite direction, northeast from the Brock Road. Confederates countered that initiative too, but in the process created an unfortunate anomaly in their position.

General Edward "Allegheny" Johnson (the nickname came from an early war victory at a place called Allegheny) led his Confederate division northeast from the Brock Road long after sundown. In the inky darkness, Johnson's staff and the van of the division emerged from thick woods into the edge of a clearing. They could see Federal campfires in the distance at what seemed to be a lower elevation, so they stopped and began to erect defensive works. By morning, the Confederate line they had fortified and extended stretched far north of the generally east-to-west axis of the troops nearer the Brock Road. This "salient" swung up and back through a broad arc that prompted some of the farm lads who fought there to bestow upon it the name "Mule Shoe."

The Mule Shoe salient, about one mile (1.6 km) deep north-to-south and half that wide, became the paramount military feature through most of the Battle of Spotsylvania. The location of the line did take advantage of high ground, and it did afford protection for Confederate supply routes farther south; but it proved to be fatally vulnerable in a tactical sense. Southern infantry erected a vast, complex array of defenses of dirt and felled trees to strengthen the salient. They also constructed traverses—interior defensive walls perpendicular to the main line—to protect against fire coming in from hostile country opposite their flanks. No fortifications, however, could extinguish the elemental defect of a salient: an enemy who broke through at any point across the entire arc immediately had at his mercy the rear of every defending unit.

General Grant's strength in numbers and materiel gave him the luxury of dictating the action. For two weeks he intermittently

General John Sedgwick, commander of the Federal VI Corps, declared "they couldn't hit an elephant at that range" just moments before a sharpshooter's bullet killed him. (Public domain)

probed at Lee's line, occasionally bludgeoning it with a massive attack. On May 9 the Army of the Potomac lost the reliable veteran commander of its VI Corps, General John Sedgwick. The corps commander's troops had been building breastworks next to the Brock Road when long-range Confederate rifle fire, from about 650 yards (600 m) away, drove them from their jobs. Sedgwick sought to inspire them to do their duty by standing tall. "They couldn't hit an elephant at that range," he said. A dull whistle announced the passage of another well-aimed bullet which whistled past. The one after that hit Sedgwick beneath his left eye and killed him instantly. He was the highest-ranking Federal officer killed during the war.

Federals probed west of the Po, where Confederates blocked them successfully, but the heaviest fighting surged back and forth across the entrenched positions in the Mule Shoe salient. On May 10, General Emory Upton, the bright young New Yorker in command of a Federal brigade, sold army headquarters on the notion of attacking a vulnerable segment of Lee's line. Upton led a dozen regiments to the edge of a wood that looked across 150 yds (135 m) of open field toward the northwest corner of the Mule Shoe. There a salient on the salient—a small bulge on the corner of the larger projection—offered an attractive target. The Federals waiting to attack dreaded the deadly fire they would face the moment they emerged from cover. "I felt my gorge rise," one of them wrote, "and my stomach and intestines shrink together in a knot … I fully realized the terrible peril I was to encounter. I looked about in the faces of the boys around me, and they told the tale of expected death. Pulling my cap down over my eyes, I stepped out."

Upton's direct assault surprised the Confederates—Georgians under General George Doles. It burst over the works, captured several hundred Southerners, and seemed poised to rupture the whole Mule Shoe position; but Confederate reinforcements hurriedly sealed the shoulder of the breach, some of them led by Lee himself. Federal supports did not come forward with the same élan Upton and his men had shown. When the fighting waned at dark, the breakthrough had been repulsed.

General Grant apparently considered Upton's success as admonitory. In the Wilderness, all of Grant's efforts to maneuver against Lee had been less than successful, and he wound up with both of the Union flanks turned and shattered. Now Upton had gone straight ahead. Perhaps the solution was simply to overwhelm the outnumbered Confederates? On May 12, Grant launched an immense assault intended to do just that. The immediate result was the heaviest day of fighting at Spotsylvania and one of the most intense hand-to-hand combats of the war. In the longer term, Grant's preliminary success on the 12th probably convinced him to adopt the notion of full-scale, head-on frontal assaults that led to vast and futile effusions of blood over the next few weeks.

Through the night of May 11–12, Federal troops marshaled opposite the northeast face of the Mule Shoe. Relentless rain and a pitch-black night complicated their preparations (one general called the result an "exquisitely ludicrous scene'), but by 4:30 AM a force of about 25,000 men had consolidated into a dense mass, ready to attack. General Winfield Scott Hancock sent them forward in what would prove to be the most successful assault of its kind by Federals during the entire war in Virginia. Hancock's leadership and the men's bravery contributed to the attack's initial success, but it also benefited from two bits of happenstance: in

Modern aerial view of Spotsylvania Court House Battlefield, looking southeast from above the Federal lines toward the Bloody Angle. The Confederate position stood at the edge of the trees beyond the field. The modern road winds down the shoulders of the Mule Shoe salient.

a dreadful stroke of bad timing, the Confederate artillery had been withdrawn from the Mule Shoe to be ready in case Grant moved eastward; and the rain and humidity had rendered most of the Confederate infantry's weapons inoperative.

The noise of the gathering enemy had been audible all night to Confederates (McHenry Howard said it sounded "like distant falling water or machinery"), and they had scrambled to get the artillery back in position. When the attackers approached, they made an incomparable target for canister or other artillery rounds—rolling forward in a wide, deep formation, impossible to miss. Most of the Confederate guns scurrying back toward the nose of the Mule Shoe, however, arrived just in time to

For hours the combatants struggled at hand-to-hand range, separated only by fortifications made of earth and wood. (Public domain)

be captured without firing a round. When the Southern infantry leveled muskets and pulled triggers, the commander of the famous old "Stonewall Brigade" expected the results he had seen many times before: volleys that knocked down the enemy in windrows and halted the assailants' momentum. But "instead of the leaping line of fire and the sharp crack of the muskets," General James A. Walker wrote in dismay, "came the pop! pop! pop! of exploding caps as the hammer fell upon them. Their powder was damp!" The military rubric, "Keep your powder dry," belonged to earlier wars fought with flintlock muskets. This affair on May 12, 1864 was the only major instance in which damp powder affected tactical events during the Civil War.

The Federal tide swept over the strong works at the nose of the Mule Shoe and roared on southward for several hundred yards. Then the chaos and disorientation, often as incumbent upon military success as upon military failure, dissolved the momentum. Desperate Confederates, some led by General Lee in person (as on May 6 and May 10), knit together new lines across the Mule Shoe and up its sides. By dint of intense, costly fighting they pushed Hancock's Federals back to the outer edge of the northern tip of the works. By then both sides had exhausted their initiative and the swirling fighting dissolved into a deadly, bloody, close encounter across the entrenchments. For 20 hours the contending forces occupied either side of a gentle bend in the works that stretched for about 160 yards (145 m), making it forever famous as "the Bloody Angle"—a *nom de guerre* christened with the blood of hundreds of soldiers.

The Bloody Angle was made possible by the tall, thick earthworks, new to the war in this campaign. No one could have fought for more than a few minutes over the kind of primitive trenches in use only a few months before. The nose of the Mule Shoe featured embattlements made of tree trunks laid lengthwise, sometimes two parallel rows with dirt between. Dirt piled over the bulk of the fortification made it impenetrable by either bullets or shells. The ditch behind the works was deep enough to require a firing step for defenders to see to fire, through a space between the main wall and a head log perched above it.

About 2,000 men from South Carolina and Mississippi clung to the south face of the works. Far more Federals from the VI and II Corps threatened the Bloody Angle from the north, but numbers mattered little in that narrow front. Most Union troops went to ground behind the lip of a draw about 40 yds (37 m) north of the works; others lay directly behind the north edge of the contested line. Brave men of both sides leaped atop the works to fire a round then drop back, if they survived. Others threw bayoneted rifles across like harpoons. A steady rain added misery to terror. The trenches filled with water "as bloody as if it flowed from an abattoir."

A Confederate called the scene "a perfect picture of gloom, destruction and death—a very Golgotha of horrors." A Federal general who visited the scene described the results of a fire so intense and long-continued "that the brush and logs were cut to pieces and whipped into basket-stuff ... men's flesh was torn from the bones and the bones shattered." Toward midnight of May 12–13, an oak tree 22 inches (56 cm) thick fell. It had been hit not by a cannonball, but by countless thousands of bullets, which gradually nibbled their way through its dense bole.

Just before dawn on May 13, the Confederate survivors finally received orders to abandon the Bloody Angle and fall back to a new line drawn across the base of the Mule Shoe—where Lee's position probably should have been formed from the outset. A Northerner who visited the newly won position at the nose of the salient left a graphic description of the place's horrors: "Horses and men chopped into hash by the bullets ... appearing ... like piles of jelly ... The logs in the breastworks were shattered into splinters ... We had not only shot down an army, but also a forest." In the aftermath of "this most desperate struggle of the war," one Mississippian who survived admitted that the tension and dread of the ordeal had shattered their nervous systems. Once they reached safe ground, the weary veterans simply "sat down on the wet ground and wept. Not silently, but vociferously and long."

Through the period May 13–17, the Federal army slipped steadily eastward, then southeastward, extending toward and around the Confederate right. This tactical measure foreshadowed Grant's strategic agenda for the next month, during which a crablike sliding movement to the southeast sought always to get closer to Richmond than Lee's army. Already he had unleashed Sheridan's cavalry to raid toward the Southern capital. The raiders did not get into Richmond, but they did kill the Confederacy's incomparable cavalry leader, General J. E. B. Stuart, in fighting around Yellow Tavern. Stuart had said "I had rather die than be whipped." Lee would miss his skill in screening and reconnaissance functions.

Although fighting flared all across the lines with regularity, the next major Federal attempt did not come until May 18. On that morning, Grant launched another massive frontal assault against Lee's troops in their strongly entrenched new lines across the base of the Mule Shoe—a position that came to be called "Lee's Last Line." Upton's head-on attack on May 10 had worked; so had the Hancock onslaught on May 12; perhaps what was needed was simply to bludgeon Lee. This time, though, Confederate cannon stood ready. Without needing much help from supporting infantry, they slaughtered Grant's attackers without the least difficulty or danger.

The Army of the Potomac recoiled after heavy losses, never having come close to their enemies. As General Meade wrote wearily to his wife the next day, after the thorough repulse "even Grant thought it useless to [continue to] knock our heads against a brick wall." Most Southern infantry hardly mentioned the event in their letters and diaries, the repulse having been so easy that it required "but little participation of our infantry." A Confederate artillery colonel wrote regretfully that the Yankee infantry "*wouldn't charge* with any spirit." In the words of a boy from Richmond, "the Union troops broke and fled."

To the North Anna and the James

Fighting on May 19 at the Harris Farm, northeast of the old salient position and beyond the Ni River, brought to a close two weeks of steady combat. Grant moved southeast in his continuing efforts to intrude between Lee and Richmond and force battle on his own terms. The two armies clashed across and around the North Anna River, midway between Spotsylvania and Richmond, on May 23–27. They waged no pitched engagement during that time, but jockeyed steadily for position.

The river, running roughly perpendicular to the Federal line of advance, offered only three usable crossings. The left (northern) bank of the stream at the fords on the eastern and western edges of the battlefield commanded the right bank, making it possible for Grant to force troops across. At Ox Ford in the middle, ground made the Confederates masters of the locale. Nonchalantly, almost indifferently, Grant pushed his columns across on each flank, giving Lee a golden opportunity to defeat either side in detail. The river and its difficult fords markedly complicated Federal options, to Lee's advantage.

In 1862 or early 1863, such circumstances would have yielded a thorough thrashing for Grant. In May 1864, however, Lee did not have the means to gather in the toothsome prize. All three of his corps commanders were out of action, and a temporary illness had almost prostrated Lee himself. He could only seethe from his cot: "We must strike them a blow—we must never let them pass us again—we must strike them a blow."

Grant steered his army southeast once more, from the North Anna River toward Totopotomoy Creek, ever closer to Richmond. Lee's customary interposition kept nudging the Federals eastward even as

Union engineer troops at work on the banks of the North Anna River, where Lee stymied Grant for four days in late May 1864. (Public domain)

General Evander M. Law's Alabama troops slaughtered attacking Federals at Cold Harbor. "It was not war," Law wrote, "it was murder." (Public domain)

they pressed south. Steady but desultory fighting at Totopotomoy led Grant toward scenes familiar from the earlier campaigns around Richmond.

By June 2 the armies were concentrating around Cold Harbor, where Lee's first great victory had been won on June 27, 1862 in the Battle of Gaines' Mill. The Confederate line that was hurriedly entrenched at the beginning of June 1864 ran right through the old battlefield; some of the 1864 fighting of greatest intensity would rage where the same armies had jousted two years before. A Northern newspaperman described the Southern entrenchments as "intricate, zig-zagged lines within lines, lines protecting flanks of lines ... a maze and labyrinth of works within works and works without works."

On June 3, weary of being blocked at every turn and always inclined toward brutally direct action, Grant simply sent forward tens of thousands of men right into that formidable warren of defenses, and into the muzzles of rifles wielded by toughened veterans. The young Northerners obliged to participate in this disaster at Cold Harbor knew what the result would be. A member of General Grant's staff noticed them pinning to their uniforms pieces of paper bearing their names and home places, so that their bodies would not go unidentified. In very short order on that late-spring morning, 7,000 Union soldiers fell to Confederate musketry without any hope of success.

A Federal from New Hampshire wrote bluntly: "It was undoubtedly the greatest and most inexcusable slaughter of the whole war ... It seemed more like a volcanic blast than a battle ... The men went down in rows, just as they marched in the ranks, and so many at a time that those in rear of them thought they were lying down." General Emory Upton, who had been so successful at Rappahannock Station and Spotsylvania with carefully planned attacks, wrote on June 4 that he was "disgusted" with the generalship displayed. "Our men have ... been foolishly and wantonly sacrificed," he wrote bitterly; "thousands of lives might have been spared by the exercise of a little skill."

Some Southerners dealing out death from behind their entrenchments around Cold Harbor blanched at the carnage, but a boy from Alabama reflected on what was being inflicted upon his country and admitted that "an indescribable feeling of pleasure courses through my veins upon surveying these heaps of the slain." A pronouncement by that Alabamian's brigade commander, General Evander M. Law, has been the most often-cited summary of Cold Harbor. "It was not war," Law mused, "it was murder."

The bloodshed northeast of Richmond settled into steady, but deadly, trench warfare for the week after June 3. Rotting corpses from the hopeless assault spread a suffocating stench across both lines; flies and other insects bedeviled the front-line troops; sniping between the lines inflicted steady casualties and made life difficult. Troops who had been scornful of digging earthworks earlier in the war now entrenched eagerly. Soon they had constructed elaborate lines and forts that stretched for miles across the countryside.

By the time of the slaughter at Cold Harbor, troops in both armies had become convinced of the value of field fortifications. They soon constructed elaborate lines that stretched for many miles. This view depicts a fort on the line around Petersburg. (Public domain)

Much of the 10 months of war that remained to be fought in Virginia would feature such horrors, but the site of most of those operations would be south of the James River. On June 12, Grant began carefully to extract substantial components of his army from the trenches and move them southward toward a crossing of the river. In managing that successful maneuver, Grant skilfully and thoroughly stole a march on General Lee, and achieved his most dramatic large-scale coup of 1864. Soldiers would continue to battle in the outskirts of Richmond for the rest of the war, but the focus of operations henceforth would move below the James to the environs of Petersburg.

Petersburg besieged

For 10 months, the primary armies in the Virginia Theater of war struggled for control of Petersburg, Virginia. They fought pitched battles for possession of key roads and rail lines; they covered the surrounding countryside with massive forts and entrenchments; and Federals fired artillery into the city. The war came to Petersburg initially, however, not with a mighty roar, but in a slowly building rhythm.

General Benjamin F. Butler's 35,000-man Army of the James posed the earliest threat to the city when it landed at Bermuda Hundred on May 4, 1864. Because the omnipotent Federal navy could land Butler's troops with impunity, they found themselves unopposed and only eight miles (13 km) northeast of Petersburg. Confederate General P. G. T. Beauregard inherited the difficult task of knitting together the sparse and disparate units in the vicinity to keep Butler in check.

The Federal general's paramount goal was Richmond, but he turned first toward Petersburg. Although steadily outnumbered by odds of three-to-one, Beauregard managed to thwart Butler in four actions between May 9 and May 22 at Port Walthall Junction, Swift Creek, Chester Station, and Drewry's Bluff. The Confederates benefited immeasurably from Butler's ineptitude, timidity, and contentiousness with his own subordinates. By May 22, Butler had given up and begun to entrench the neck of the Bermuda Hundred peninsula. In the memorable phrase of a disgusted General U. S. Grant, this left Butler's force "as completely shut off from further operations ... as if it had been in a bottle strongly corked."

On June 9, Butler tried again. He sent 6,500 men from inside the corked bottle to capture Petersburg, which lay almost entirely unprotected and apparently within easy reach. The Federal cavalry swung around to come in from the south while their infantry mates went at the town from the northeast. They were repulsed in a desperate fight that became famous as "The Battle of Old Men and Young Boys." An array of citizens beyond the outer limits of military age (ranging in age from at least 14 to 61), ill-armed and untrained, threw themselves in the path of the invaders—and turned them back. One veteran battery arrived in time to play a crucial role in the narrow margin of victory. Nearly a hundred of the civilians became casualties as they saved their hometown. Anne Banister was standing on the porch of her home with her mother and sister when a wagon brought up "my father's lifeless body shot through the head, his gray hair dabbled in blood." On the evening of June 9, "universal mourning was over the town, for the young and old were lying dead in many homes."

By the time the rag-tag civilian assemblage had held Petersburg, U. S. Grant had decided to devote his main army to the task of capturing the city. The incredibly costly repulse of his troops at Cold Harbor on June 3 had eroded even Grant's oblivious determination. Taking Petersburg would sever most of the roads and railroads heading to Richmond, thus cutting the Confederate capital off from the rest of the Confederacy. On June 12, Grant began deftly to disengage major units of the Army of the Potomac from its trenches and move it by stages to the James River. On the 14th the crossing began, in part on transports and in part by way of an enormous pontoon bridge, more than 2,000 ft (600 m) in length, that was one of the engineering wonders of the war.

General Robert E. Lee's remarkable ability to divine his enemy's intentions stood him in good stead in many a campaign, but it deserted him in early June. Grant slipped away from Lee's presence without the Confederate chieftain learning of the move. When Beauregard reported the arrival south of the James of portions of the main enemy army, Lee discounted the news. Beauregard's tendency to concoct visionary schemes and embrace implausible notions contributed to Lee's uncertainty, but Grant thoroughly and unmistakably stole a march on his adversary. The result was a three-day span during which Petersburg stood almost defenseless against a Northern horde.

One of the war's great marvels is that Grant's men did not simply march into Petersburg during June 15–18. They surely would have done so had they not been enervated by the bloodletting of the previous month. On the 15th, more than 15,000 Northerners faced barely 2,000 Southerners. The defenders spread themselves in thin, widely separated clusters among works begun in 1862 to protect the city. Late on the 15th, a portion of that line fell to attacking Federals. "Petersburg,"

Southerners called General Benjamin F. Butler "Beast Butler" for his attitudes toward civilians in occupied New Orleans in 1862. In 1864, Butler fumbled hopelessly in his operations around Petersburg. (Public domain)

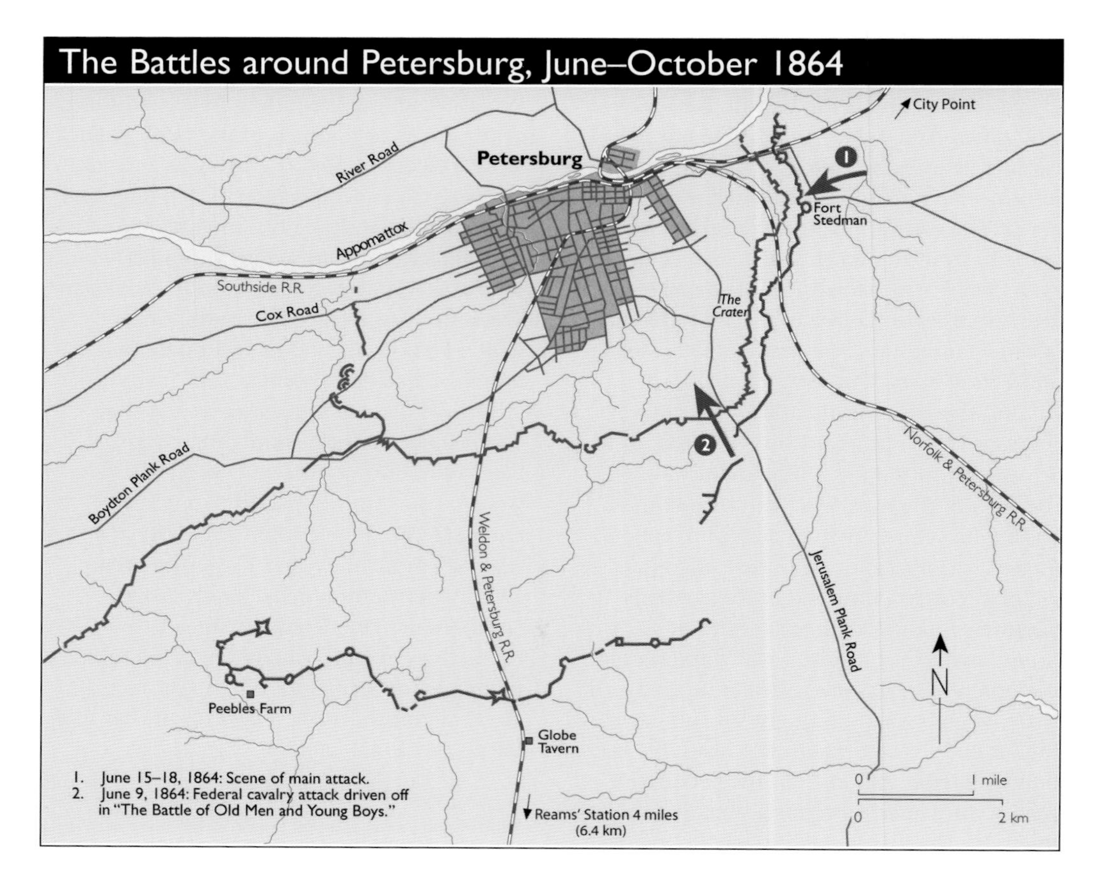

For 10 months beginning in mid-June 1864, the war in Virginia swung around the pivot of Petersburg. The roads and railroads leading through Petersburg to Richmond became the Confederate capital's final lifeline. For weeks in early June the city lay virtually undefended, but the first Federal raiders suffered a repulse at the hands of old men and youngsters beyond the age limits for regular army service. During June 15–18, uncoordinated attacks failed to break into Petersburg despite being opposed by only a tiny handful of Southern troops. Thereafter the fighting became a deadly struggle for the railroads. Grant pushed columns west, gradually closing off Confederate use of the Jerusalem Plank Road, then the Weldon Railroad, and eventually the Boydton Plank Road. If he could reach the South Side Railroad, Petersburg and Richmond would be strangled. The winter of 1864–65 closed in before Grant could accomplish that final measure.

Beauregard wrote, "was clearly at the mercy of the Federal commander."

For two more days, Grant's troops swarmed around Petersburg without making a decisive move. Early on June 18, the first men from Lee's Army of Northern Virginia finally arrived, and Lee himself reached the town before noon. The Confederates bought time by abandoning their outer works on the 18th, leaving the first Federal attack to dissipate in a confusing complex of empty trenches.

When the blue-clad legions reformed and moved forward again, they attacked without concert—and without success. The First Maine Heavy Artillery, which Grant had extracted from a cozy post in the quiet forts around Washington and sent into the line with muskets, was butchered. More than 630 of the Maine men fell in an utterly hopeless assault. During the entire Civil War, no regiment suffered as many losses in one engagement. One of the minority who survived unscathed described the experience: "The earth was literally torn up with iron and lead ... human courage, flesh, and bone were struggling with an

The brave but hopeless charge of the 1st Maine Heavy Artillery at Petersburg, June 18, 1864. The Maine unit lost more men here in a single battle than any other regiment on either side during the entire war. (Painting by Don Troiani, www.historicalartprints.com)

impossibility ... In ten minutes those who were not slaughtered had returned." The next morning a dense fog lifted to reveal a "field of slaughter, strewn thick with the blue-coated bodies ... decomposing in the fierce rays of a Southern sun."

While the bitter Maine veteran gazed across a field covered with his friends' bodies, major elements of Lee's Army of Northern Virginia were filing steadily into the defenses. Those sturdy troops would not be routed from their entrenchments by any kind of frontal assault. Petersburg had been saved, and for more than nine months would stand, with Richmond, as the last major Confederate citadel in Virginia.

The Crater

When the wretchedly managed Federal assaults of June 15–18 ended in an ineffectual welter of blood, Grant faced the necessity to begin a siege. He had lost more than 10,000 men in the awkward attempt to batter his way into Petersburg, as against appreciably fewer than half as many Confederate casualties. With characteristic determination, Grant quickly arranged to extend his lines southwestward across Lee's front. His purpose in this and several subsequent initiatives was to snap Southern railroads and other lines of communication and supply. At the same time, his almost limitless resources in men and materiel would benefit from ever-longer front lines. Eventually the limited Confederate strength would be stretched to the breaking point. Execution of those two initiatives constituted the story of the next nine months.

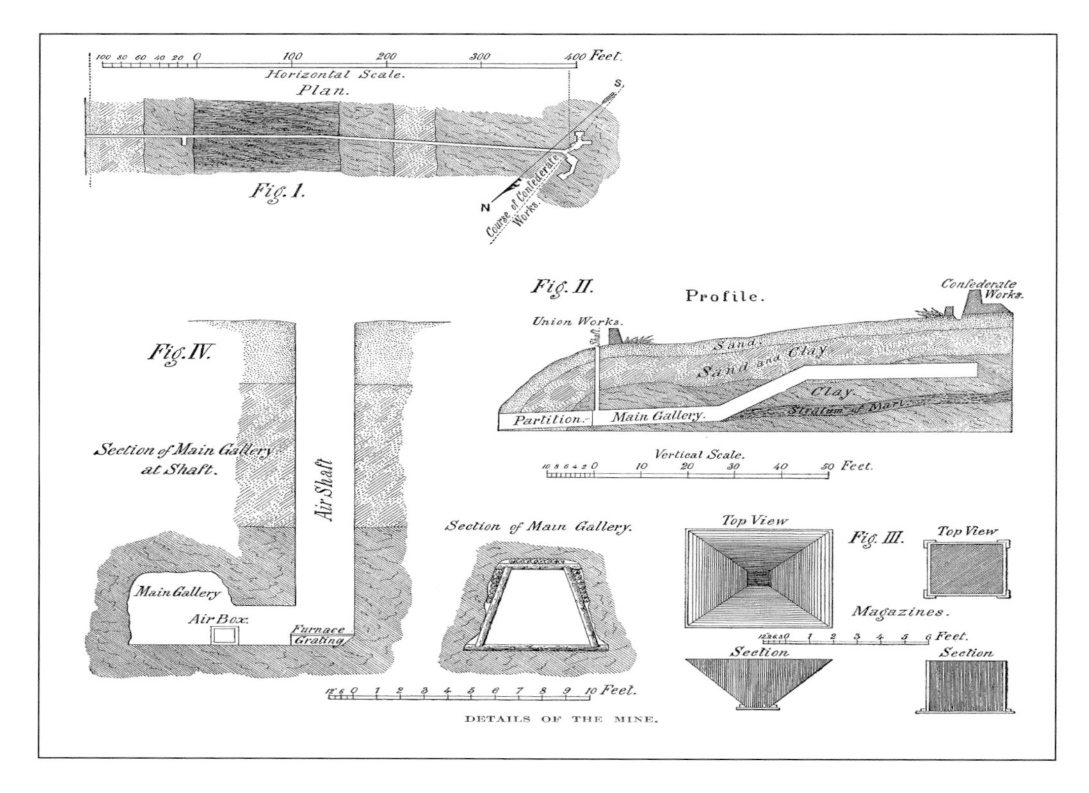

The sturdy coal miners who dug the tunnel between the lines faced considerable danger and discomfort even before it was packed with 8,000 lbs (3, 629 kg) of powder. Their ingenious system for drawing fresh air into the tunnel made the project possible. (Public domain)

Grant's first move of his left beyond Lee's right came on June 21. The reliable II Corps, under the magnificent leadership of General Winfield Scott Hancock, moved across the Jerusalem Plank Road, permanently denying that artery to the Confederates, and on toward the Weldon Railroad. Lee could not surrender the vital rail link without a fight. He sent two divisions out to intercept Hancock's force. The tactical result was stunning. The glorious old Federal II Corps folded and ran in the face of a smaller force, losing 2,500 men, the vast majority of them as prisoners of war.

This embarrassing result, which could not have been imagined under any circumstances from that seasoned formation a few months earlier, highlighted the condition of Grant's army. It had been bled so thoroughly, and enervated so completely, that it had lost its hard-won and long-held prowess. Most of the army's field-grade officers, company officers, and non-commissioned officers lay moldering in graves between the Rapidan and James Rivers, or languishing wounded in facilities along the east coast.

The unmistakable historical record shows that accepting about 200,000 combined casualties in getting to Richmond did end the war in a year of bloodshed. A minority opinion suggests that the immutable advantages of terrain and strategic imperatives available to the Federal cause around Petersburg would have set a far more desirable stage upon which to invoke elements of the military art. By the time the Army of the Potomac reached that advantageous ground in 1864, however, the army retained only a barely recognizable shadow of its former might. The months to come would feature operations in the image of the Weldon Railroad.

General Winfield Scott Hancock's superb leadership had made the Federal II Corps into a redoubtable force. (Public domain)

Through the summer of 1864, Grant intermittently pushed his left farther west, and Lee countered on his right. Most of the soldiers' energies, however, went into work with shovels rather than with rifles. A warren of forts and redoubts and trenches sprang up and ambled across the Virginia countryside. Men fought from behind works of wood and dirt, and lived in "bombproofs," as they called their rude homes hollowed out in the earth and reinforced with timber.

One of the war's most remarkable episodes, the product of an amazing engineering feat, grew out of the stalemate imposed by impregnable fortifications. Attacking a deeply entrenched enemy afforded little hope of success, against a guarantee of staggering casualties. A regiment recruited in coal-mining country, the 48th Pennsylvania Infantry, conceived the notion of digging a tunnel far beneath the earth's surface that would lead under the Confederate line, which then could be blown to smithereens. The Pennsylvanians undertook the novel project with a great deal of energy and ingenuity. They modified ration boxes to use for removing the dirt. They sent parties out to cut timber to shore up the excavation. They fabricated a complex but clever means to exhaust bad air from the

The fight for control of the Crater developed into a savage hand-to-hand struggle. (Public domain)

lengthening tunnel and bring in fresh air through a wooden conduit. After three weeks of labor, the miners had completed a tunnel that ran 511 ft (156 m) and ended squarely beneath the main enemy line. For 10 days they dug a lateral chamber and then packed it full of gunpowder—four tons of it. They planned to blow up the massive charge at dawn on July 30.

The Pennsylvanian soldier-miners had achieved an incredible success, but the Federal military hierarchy had not done nearly as well preparing to capitalize on the fruits of their labor. General Ambrose E. Burnside, who had failed so egregiously at Fredericksburg in 1862, was back with the army in command of the Federal IX Corps and responsible for the sector where the 48th had dug so diligently. He decided to assign his well-trained but untested all-black division to exploit the gap to be made by the explosion. General Meade refused to let Burnside use the black troops as the first wave because he knew that, if they took heavy losses, he would be pilloried by politicians and journalists. Burnside chose (by the mindless expedient of drawing straws) to substitute the least effective of his white divisions, commanded by the inept—and perhaps drunken—General James H. Ledlie.

Exploding the mine involved moments of high drama. An officer of the 48th lit the long, long fuse at 3:00 AM and thousands of men in blue waited in breathless silence for the explosion. Thousands of Confederates in deadly danger dozed in innocence. Nothing happened. By 4:15 AM it had become apparent that nothing was going to happen without intervention. Two brave Pennsylvanians, Lieutenant Jacob Douty (a doughty fellow indeed) and Sergeant Harry Reese, crawled into the long, dark mine to investigate. They found that the fuse had failed at one of its several splices, relit it, and scurried to safety. Finally, at 4:45 AM the "earth trembled for miles around," as a Virginia soldier put it, under the echoes of

HEADQUARTERS OF GENERAL GRANT AND BASE OF SUPPLIES, CITY POINT, ON THE JAMES RIVER. FROM AN OIL-PAINTING.

a mighty explosion. The blast killed or wounded nearly 300 South Carolinians.

When Smith Lipscomb, who survived, tumbled out of the air and landed on his feet, his "thies [thighs] felt like they were almost shivered." Lipscomb thought that he must have been badly crippled, but a Federal volley "convinced me I was not as badly hurt as I thought I was," he recalled later. The injured man staggered back under cover and began rubbing his painful legs. Before long he had found a rifle and began shooting at the enemy. The carnage continued until Smith "saw the blood run down [a] little drain ditch several feet."

Ledlie's troops dashed forward toward the breach and gazed in awe at a chasm about 170 feet long, 80 feet wide, and 30 feet deep (50 m × 25 m × 10 m). While they stared at the place known ever since as "the Crater," Confederates behind the gap and on either side began to rally. Federal reinforcements pushed into the Crater and beyond, but fire from either flank limited their penetration.

(Public domain)

General Lee pulled Southern reinforcements from points all around his front to use in re-establishing his line. For several hours, an opening blown in the Confederate position beckoned Federals to lunge through and capture the city just beyond. Eventually Burnside received permission to commit the black division to the fight, but long after the crucial moment for which those troops had been trained. The black soldiers simply added to the chaos in the muddy, bloody Crater.

As Confederate units closed in, Federals in the Crater became defenders instead of attackers. Artillery shells, some of them from newly deployed high-angle mortars, exploded above the Crater and flung shards into its corners. The Confederate charge that retook the position erupted over the lip of the Crater and surged through its midst in hand-to-hand combat that turned the pit into "one seething cauldron of struggling, dying men." General J. C. C. Sanders of Alabama, who commanded a brigade at the scene, wrote that Southern guns "literally mowed down the enemy piling up Yankees and Negroes on each other." Confederate artillerist Frank Huger used similar language: "our men literally butchered them." A Massachusetts officer described the crowded situation inside the Crater as so tight that "many of those killed were held in a standing position until jostled to the ground."

A conflict in which slavery had become a steadily more significant issue had now reached a point where former slaves fought directly on the front line for their freedom and that of their brothers.

When the last Federal survivor dashed back to the lines beyond the Crater, an unusually dramatic battle ended and a dazzling opportunity had disappeared. The Union army lost 4,000 men on July 30; the Confederates about 1,500. General Grant removed Burnside and Ledlie from their commands, and summarized the Crater in regretful benediction: "It was the saddest affair

I have witnessed in the war." There would be no other chance to go straight at Petersburg until the war's final week. For Grant, it was back to striking westward toward the railroads.

The struggle for the railroads

Ten days after the fight for the Crater, another gigantic explosion rocked the region. In the war's most dramatic incident of espionage and sabotage, Confederate agent John Maxwell blew up a time bomb on a barge full of explosives at Grant's headquarters complex at City Point, a few miles below Petersburg. The result, a colonel wrote to his wife, was "terrible—awful—terrific." The blast and secondary explosions killed 50 Federals, destroyed several structures, and did millions of dollars' worth of damage. The North's seemingly bottomless industrial capacity easily replaced the losses, but Southerners had occasion to cheer a daring and dramatic act.

Supplies and their transportation took center stage through the summer and fall of 1864. Railroads and wagon roads leading into Petersburg from the west and southwest sustained Lee's army around the city and also supplied sustenance for both troops and civilians around the national capital, 30 miles (48 km) northward. Lee had to fight to keep those lines open. Grant welcomed the chance to close them, and to meet Lee's dwindling strength in the open, away from the powerful fortifications that neutralized the armies' differences in strength.

In mid-August, Grant moved again toward the Weldon Railroad. This time he stuck there. On the 18th, Warren's Federal V Corps effected a lodgment near Globe Tavern on the railroad. Two Confederate brigades hurried to the site and routed an isolated Union detachment, but did not have nearly enough strength to drive Warren away. The next day a further Confederate effort, this time in more strength, again achieved localized success. A Virginian fighting near Globe Tavern called it "the warmest place" that he ever had been in, "subjected to fire from the front, right flank, & rear all at the same time."

General Gouverneur K. Warren led his Federal V Corps in several sweeps south and west from Petersburg, steadily extending the lines and stretching Lee's Confederates toward breaking point. (Public domain)

In fact, it was Warren's right flank that came under the greatest pressure. He lost most of two seasoned regiments as prisoners, and the situation seemed desperate for a brief interval. Reinforcements enabled Warren to hold fast on August 19, and on August 21 he handily repulsed a series of Southern attacks. In one of them, a bullet tore through both of General John C. C. Sanders' thighs and he bled to death. He had reached his twenty-fourth birthday four months before. A few days later his sister back in Alabama wrote to a surviving brother of her wrenching loss. Fannie Sanders described dreaming of John every night, then awakening to the living nightmare of the truth. "Why! Oh why, was not my worthless life taken instead of that useful one!" Fannie cried. "I have been blinded with tears." Families on both sides of the Potomac had abundant cause for grief.

The fight for Globe Tavern and the railroad cost some 4,300 Union casualties, and 2,300 Confederate.

With a new anchor on the Weldon Railroad, Grant's lines stretched farther westward, requiring Lee to match the expansion, despite the direly thinning Southern resources. Grant immediately sent his once-powerful II Corps right down the Weldon line to destroy it as far south as possible. He could not permanently occupy that zone south of Globe Tavern, but he welcomed the chance to destroy more Southern transportation. The II Corps had been eviscerated in May, though, and repeated its poor showing of June in the Battle of Reams' Station on August 24–25.

Confederate General A. P. Hill led out a mixed reaction force of eight infantry brigades drawn from various portions of the line, forming what in later wars would be called a "battle group," brought together for a specific mission. The infantry joined with General Wade Hampton's Southern cavalry to surround and batter the Federals, who put up only a feeble resistance. General Hancock, the superb commander of the Union corps, rode among his men, waving his hat and his sword, shouting "For God's sake do not run!" His bravery accomplished little. Hill inflicted about 2,700 casualties, many of them captured, and lost only 700 men himself. The new Union bulwark at Globe Tavern, however, remained intact.

During September 14–17, Hampton's mounted troops executed one of the most successful raids of the war—"the Beefsteak Raid." About 4,000 Confederate horsemen dashed far behind the Union army and rustled a huge herd of beef cattle from under their enemies' noses. Hungry Southern troopers found most of the cattle guard "cozily sleeping in their tents." Hampton lost only a few dozen men and returned with 300 human prisoners and 2,500 cattle. The hunger rampant in the South by this time made the beef a tantalizing prize of war.

Elsewhere, September was a bad month for Confederate arms in Georgia, where Atlanta fell to General William T. Sherman,

On September 29, a determined Federal assault captured Fort Harrison on Lee's main defensive line outside Richmond. (Public domain)

and in Virginia's Shenandoah Valley. Late in the month Federal initiatives also brought on some of the heaviest fighting of the year along the Richmond–Petersburg lines. Between September 29 and October 7, 1864, intense action erupted below Richmond and north of the James, and also around Petersburg west of the new Union establishment at Globe Tavern. Grant had attacked unsuccessfully north of the James twice before near Deep Bottom, in coordination with his offensives around Petersburg. This new effort fell with impressive might on the Confederate

General U. S. Grant's dogged determination dictated the nature of the 10-month-long investment of Richmond and Petersburg. (Author's collection)

defensive line around Chaffin's Bluff and New Market Heights. Federal attackers ran headlong into a linchpin of the defensive complex at Fort Harrison, and captured it at the climax of a bloody assault. A New Hampshire soldier described the deadly work: "Our men fall riddled with bullets; great gaps are rent in our ranks as the shells cut their way through us, or burst in our midst; a solid shot or a shell ... will bore straight through ten or twenty men; here are some men literally cut in two, others yonder are blown to pieces."

The cost of the success, which included the death of General Hiram Burnham, commander of an attacking brigade, drained away momentum in the Union ranks. Once again a temporary advantage wilted for lack of immediate exploitation. Lee directed a counterattack in person the next day, hoping to retake Fort Harrison, but it failed. The Southern leader faced the necessity of carving out a new position closer to Richmond. Fighting in the area continued intermittently for a week, killing General John Gregg of the famous Texas Confederate brigade on Darbytown Road on October 7, but no decision resulted. Confederate territory on the Richmond–Petersburg lines continued to shrink.

While Lee struggled to maintain his position outside Richmond, Grant simultaneously renewed his pressure south and west of Petersburg. General Warren again commanded a mixed force vectored toward that sensitive Confederate flank. His target this time was the Boydton Plank Road, west of Globe Tavern. Beyond that road ran a truly significant target—the South Side Railroad, Lee's last rail link into Petersburg. Warren found early success, but Confederate counter-measures directed by General A. P. Hill yielded results by now familiar: tactical victories for the Confederates against dispirited Yankees; but strategic success for Grant in the form of farther extension of his lines to the west. On September 30 and October 1, the troops fought fiercely on the Peebles Farm and the Jones Farm. Hill's men held Warren away from the Boydton Plank Road, and far short of the South Side Railroad, inflicting about 3,000 losses as against 1,300 Confederate casualties. When the smoke cleared, however, Unionist forts and earthworks had begun to sprout in this new sector.

In late October, the final major Federal effort to westward in 1864 moved toward the same target that had eluded Warren at Peebles Farm. While the customary diversionary demonstrations unfolded near Richmond, a mighty force composed of troops from three infantry corps, supported by a strong cavalry detachment, would push once again to the Boydton Plank Road and then beyond toward the much-coveted South Side Railroad.

On October 27, General Hancock and his II Corps succeeded in brushing aside Confederate cavalry and reaching the Boydton road, breaking across it near Burgess' Mill on Hatcher's Run. In that vicinity the victorious Yankees came up against infantry and artillery in a good position. Warren's Federal V Corps floundered through tangled brush in a vain attempt to help. Meanwhile, the customary Confederate reinforcements pounded rapidly down the roads from Petersburg. Late on the 27th, those new troops attacked Hancock's men with vigor. Although they did not break the Union line, the Southerners hammered it so hard that Hancock retreated overnight and left his wounded behind. Burgess' Mill had cost him 1,800 casualties, the Confederates 1,300.

As winter spread its grip across Virginia, and major operations became impracticable, Lee's line stretched far wider than the Southern leader would have preferred. When next the weather would allow Grant to move farther west, Lee would have little chance of resisting effectually. The armies retired into watchful winter quiet in their heavily entrenched lines. Desertion increased on both sides. War-weary Confederates slipped away steadily. Even the ever-more-powerful Union armies suffered more than 7,300 desertions nationwide per month on average during 1864.

The Shenandoah Valley Campaign of 1864

In the spring of 1862, General Thomas J. "Stonewall" Jackson catapulted to lasting fame by waging a campaign in Virginia's fertile and lovely Shenandoah Valley that captured the imagination of the South and transformed the nature of the war. By turns careful and then dazzling in his maneuvers, Jackson utilized the valley's features to his own advantage. The two forks of the Shenandoah river served as moats, being crossed at only three places in 100 miles (160 km) by bridges. The Massanutten Mountain massif ran down the heart of the valley for 50 miles (80 km) as an immense bulwark and shield. The northeastern end of the valley reached a latitude north of Washington, and looked like a shotgun pointed at the Northern capital. A Unionist who fought in the region described its military character: "The Shenandoah Valley is a queer place, and it will not submit to the ordinary rules of military tactics. Operations are carried on here that Caesar or Napoleon never dreamed of. Either army can surround the other, and I believe that both can do it at the same time."

The irascible but able General Jubal A. Early fought against heavy odds in the Shenandoah Valley. General Lee called him "my bad old man." (Public domain)

As Confederate options near Richmond and Petersburg narrowed in 1864, General Lee determined to take advantage of the valley again. He sent his trusted and able lieutenant, General Jubal A. Early, to cause Jackson-like chaos in that vulnerable sector.

Significant operations had been under way in the valley for several weeks by the time Early arrived. General Grant's comprehensive plan to keep pressure up all across the Confederacy's frontiers included the dispatch of two tentacles toward the valley. General William W. Averell led an expedition in southwestern Virginia against the Virginia and Tennessee Railroad. He was successful in a stubbornly contested action at Cloyd's Mountain on May 9, 1864, but Averell's mission did not have a major direct impact on the war's main theater.

At the same time, General Franz Sigel pushed a force of some 10,000 men south up the valley (the rivers run nominally northward, so south is "up" the valley) toward the vital Confederate depot and rail junction at Staunton. The German-born Sigel offered Grant and President Lincoln more political energy than military prowess, appealing as he did to the large population of German-born immigrants living in the North. A non-German in Sigel's army described the men's "most supreme contempt for General Sigel and his crowd of foreign adventurers." Even Grant admitted that he could not "calculate on very great results" in western Virginia.

Against Sigel the Confederates mustered an army about half the size of their adversary's, led by General John C. Breckinridge, a former Vice-President of the United States and a future Confederate Secretary of War. The disparate fragments that made up Breckinridge's army included a detachment of boys who would become famous in the impending fighting, the teenaged cadets of the Virginia Military Institute (VMI). On May 15, 1864 the two small armies clashed at the crossroads village of New Market, with control of the valley at stake. A steady rain complicated the brutal business of firing muskets and cannon, holding the acrid gunsmoke close to the ground and making the battlefield an eerie stage. Men from Massachusetts, Pennsylvania, Ohio, and Connecticut peered down from a commanding crest on the Virginians pressing toward them. Colonel George S. Patton I commanded a key Southern brigade; his grandson and namesake would win fame 80 years later in a very different war.

In the midst of the Confederate line marched the 250 young cadets. Several had just turned 15 years of age. "They are only children," Breckinridge said worriedly to an aide, "and I cannot expose them to such fire." The exigencies of the moment left him no choice, and the youngsters dashed forward through sheets of lead so "withering," their commander wrote, that "it seemed impossible that any living creature could escape." The boys charged in a torrential thunderstorm across a fire-swept field so muddy that it sucked some of their shoes from their feet, then dashed into the midst of the Federal cannon. Regular troops on either side of them had played an important role, but the VMI cadets had behaved like veterans. Their youthful assault fostered a legend. Fifty-seven of them (21 percent) fell as casualties, 10 of those mortal. Among the dead lads was a grandson of Thomas Jefferson.

Breckinridge and his men chased Sigel north for miles, but the victory proved to be temporary. Breckinridge hurried across the Blue Ridge Mountains to help General Lee around Richmond. Sigel's military debits had finally outweighed his political assets and President Lincoln shelved him. General David Hunter reorganized Sigel's command and led it south again. On June 5 he destroyed a small, hurriedly assembled force led by Confederate General William E. "Grumble" Jones (the nickname being well earned on the basis of Jones's personality) in the Battle of Piedmont. Ill-disciplined Confederate cavalry failed to perform at the crisis. When Jones fell dead his rag-tag army dissolved, and for the first time during the war, a Northern force gained control of the invaluable railroad junction and warehouses of Staunton. Hunter then moved south to Lexington, burning homes as he went—some of them belonging to his own kin, who seemed to receive especially harsh treatment. Soldiers torched the home in Lexington of Virginia's former governor, John Letcher, denying the family's women and children the chance to remove even clothing from the house before it became engulfed by the flames.

When Hunter crossed the mountains and closed in on Lynchburg, another vital railhead and supply depot, General Lee determined that he must be checked. To that end, he ordered Early to lead the Second Corps of the Army of Northern Virginia westward. The corps made an obvious choice: it had been in the famed 1862 Valley Campaign under Stonewall Jackson, and many of the men lived in or near the valley. Early was an equally good choice because of his energy and determination. The fiery Virginian stood up in his stirrups while scouting the lines around Lynchburg, shook a fist at the Yankees, and bellowed his scorn

General Thomas L. Rosser commanded Confederate cavalry in the valley. Early compared him to Judas Iscariot. (Public domain)

for both his enemy and the irregular Southern troops he was replacing: "No buttermilk rangers after you now, you ... Blue Butts!" Early used the derisive term "buttermilk rangers" to refer to stragglers, especially cavalry, ranging to the rear for refreshments instead of doing their duty. His difficulties with poor cavalry would bedevil operations for the next five months.

Early's seasoned troops chased the Federals away from Lynchburg on June 17–19, 1864. Hunter's men straggled through the trackless mountains in West Virginia on a weary march that took them out of operations for weeks. Early promptly turned north and moved steadily down the entire length of the valley and into the very outskirts of Washington, DC. En route he fought an engagement on July 9 near Frederick, Maryland, on the banks of the Monocacy river. A blocking force under Federal General Lew Wallace (who would write the classic novel *Ben Hur* after the war) fought all day to retard Early's advance

The victorious charge of the youthful cadets of the Virginia Military Institute at New Market, as painted by Benjamin West Clinedinst, a postwar graduate of the Institute. (Virginia Military Institute Museum)

toward Washington. Wallace's troops eventually recoiled, but they had achieved their purpose.

President Lincoln worriedly wired to General Grant at Petersburg, urging him to come in person. Grant instead sent most of two corps of infantry to reinforce Washington—precisely the sort of result Lee had desired when he unleashed Early. Lincoln went to the forts on the

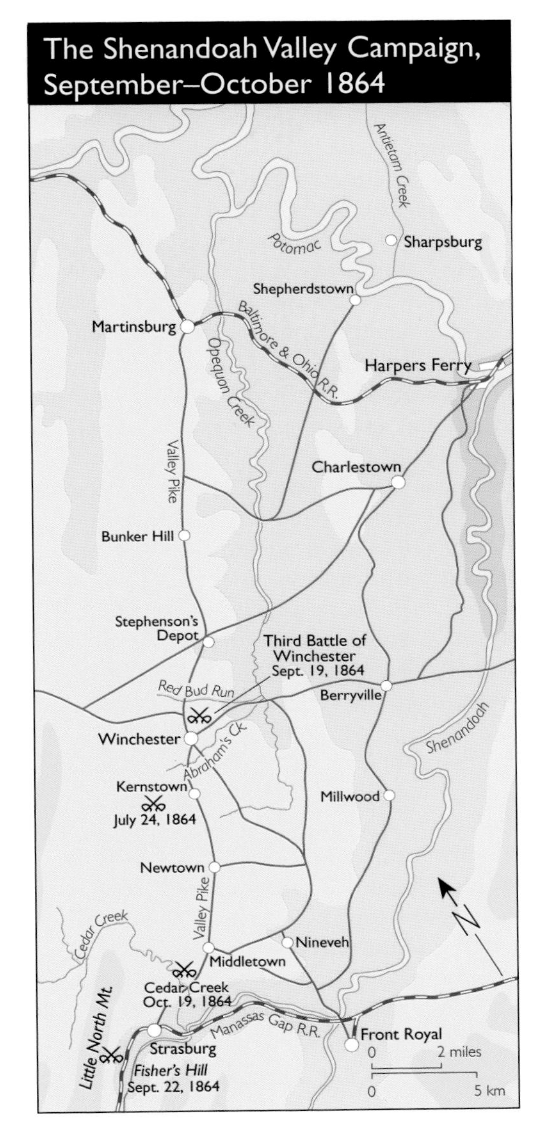

The Shenandoah Valley Campaign, September–October 1864

Although Federals outnumbered him by three-to-one, Confederate General Jubal A. Early put up a stout resistance in the northern Shenandoah Valley in the autumn of 1864. In the Battles of Third Winchester (September 19), Fisher's Hill (September 22) and Cedar Creek (October 19), the Federals suffered considerably more casualties than they inflicted on their Southern foes—but they could afford the losses and Early could not. After Cedar Creek, Confederate presence in the once-fertile valley consisted of little more than a nuisance force of cavalry and irregular troops.

line outside Washington and came under desultory long-range fire. The Confederates did not get into the capital city proper, and could not have held it had they done so. As Jubal Early commented in summary: "We haven't taken Washington, but we've scared Abe Lincoln ... !"

Union forces pursued Early to the Potomac River as he retired, then to the slopes of the Blue Ridge, and then beyond to the Shenandoah river. Early's rearguard repulsed them along the way, then savagely turned on the Federals at Kernstown on July 24, just south of Winchester. There the Confederates inflicted one of the most unmitigated thrashings of the war on their enemies, who suffered more than 1,200 casualties as against fewer than 250 Confederates lost. A few days later, General Grant sent a new commander to the Shenandoah Valley, with strong reinforcements. His instructions to General Philip H. Sheridan were to whip Early, and then to turn the beautiful valley into "a barren waste."

Despite an enormous preponderance in numbers, Sheridan had a far easier time accomplishing the "barren waste" element of his orders than he did in whipping Early. In the decisive battles of September and October, Sheridan was able to deploy more cavalry than Early had troops of all arms combined. Those cavalry, furthermore, enjoyed wide mobility on good horses, and carried weapons that dramatically out-performed the equipment available to the Southern horsemen. Early did not trust his cavalry. He had more than ample cause for queasiness, but his fractious relationship with the mounted arm only exacerbated a deadly situation. In postwar quarreling with General Thomas L. Rosser, his chief cavalry subordinate during the campaign, Early compared him to Judas Iscariot, and suggested that if Rosser were to emulate Judas and hang himself, it would be "the most creditable act" he could perform.

For more than six weeks, Sheridan followed Early's detachments hither and yon through the northern valley as the Confederates tore up the Baltimore and Ohio Railroad—a vital Federal artery—and feinted at supply depots as far north as the Potomac River. Early's energetic deployments convinced Sheridan that he faced far more enemy strength than actually existed. Finally, on September 19, Sheridan hurled two corps through a narrow canyon east of Winchester and brought Early to pitched battle.

In bitter fighting that swirled across fields and woodlots between Red Bud Run and Abraham's Creek, exploding shells took a steep toll among ranking officers. Federal General David A. Russell, an accomplished brigade commander who had graduated from West Point and served in the antebellum army, fell instantly dead when a shell fragment went through his heart. A piece of shell hit Confederate General Archibald C. Godwin in the head and killed him instantly. The highest-ranking casualty on either side was Confederate General Robert E. Rodes, perhaps the best division commander in the Virginia Theater, who also died from a shell fragment in the head.

Despite being direly outnumbered, the Southern infantry east of Winchester held their ground and inflicted staggering casualties on Sheridan's attackers. The moment of decision came from behind the sturdy defenders, northwest of the scene of the heavy fighting. A wall of Union cavalry swept into the northern outskirts of Winchester and simply overwhelmed the Confederate horsemen in front of them. Early had no choice but to collapse his outflanked main line and fight for time to get away before the enemy's mounted troops could deploy entirely behind his army. He succeeded in that effort, aided by the onset of darkness, falling back 20 miles (32 km) to a strong position at Fisher's Hill.

George S. Patton, who had done so well at New Market, fell mortally wounded by another exploding shell during the retreat. Artillery fragments reaped an especially deadly harvest of braided officers on this day. The Third Battle of Winchester extracted more than 5,000 casualties from Sheridan's attackers. Early lost 1,700 men killed and wounded. He reported 1,800 men missing, but declared that many of them were "stragglers and skulkers," not prisoners.

Twice more in the next month Early would fight Sheridan. Each time the formula would resemble that of Winchester: Early's indomitable infantry would attack successfully or bloodily repulse their enemies, then Confederate cavalry on Early's left flank would collapse and unravel the entire line.

Sheridan pressed briskly forward toward Fisher's Hill on September 20 and on the 21st he skirmished as necessary to secure the ridges opposite Early's new position. Keeping steady pressure on his outnumbered and reeling opponent made good sense. General

Early's Confederates fought Sheridan's Federals to a standstill east of Winchester on September 19, 1864, but Northern cavalry eventually overran Early's left and decided the day. (Public domain)

George Crook, who would later achieve notable success in the Indian Wars in the southwestern United States, conceived a bold plan to unhinge Early's line. Crook proposed taking his entire corps up onto the slopes of Little North Mountain, which anchored the Confederate left, then moving south until he was in a position to turn the enemy line. Sheridan cavalierly, and characteristically, claimed for himself all of the credit for this battle plan, although his own preliminary proposal had been to launch an utterly impractical frontal assault on the opposite end of the line.

On September 22, while the rest of Sheridan's army demonstrated straight ahead toward Fisher's Hill, Crook put his plan into action. It worked fabulously well, in part because Early had again positioned his unreliable cavalry at the most vulnerable segment of his position. The Confederates reeled southward again in total disarray, losing prisoners and cannon as they went. Early's defeated fragments did not stop until they had scampered more than 50 miles (80 km). An onlooker heard a weary Confederate chanting a home-spun ditty that began, "Old Jube Early's gone up the spout." Early blamed his army for the rout. When a passing soldier yelled irreverently at the army commander, Early spat back, "Fisher's Hill ... ," believing that the very name of that embarrassment was opprobrium enough.

Sheridan had cause to believe that he had forever removed Early's little army from serious consideration, and set about destroying the valley systematically. His men killed thousands of animals, burned countless barns and mills, and destroyed

Colonel George S. Patton I, grandfather of the Second World War general, commanded a brigade at Winchester until a shell mortally wounded him. (Public domain)

crops everywhere. The vandalism loosened or destroyed the reins of discipline in some instances, and Unionists went beyond warfare on agriculture to burn houses and savage civilian women in what Virginians called "The Burning." Ironically, the region most heavily affected included one of the largest concentrations of unflinching pacifists on the continent, most of them Mennonites or Dunkards; their buildings burned as briskly as anyone else's.

Southern cavalrymen, many of them watching their own homes aflame, could not stem the onslaught, but they took the chance to execute groups of enemy arsonists when they cornered them. War never treads gently, especially civil war, but the American strife in the 1860s had been amazingly civilized—until the fall of 1864. Rosser's enraged Confederate cavalry eventually stretched too far from infantry support and suffered a resounding beating on October 9 at Tom's Brook by Union cavalry under Generals George A. Custer, Wesley Merritt, and Alfred T. A. Torbert.

Incredibly, Early pushed back northward once more soon after Tom's Brook, a phoenix risen from the ashes, and by mid-October had again reached the vicinity of Fisher's Hill. Sheridan had concluded that his foe had been permanently vanquished, but the

Starting on October 6, Sheridan's Federals systematically burned out the Shenandoah Valley. (Public domain)

small Southern force launched against him one of the most amazing surprise assaults of the war. Lee had sent Early reinforcements from Richmond, among them some of the army's most dependable units. Confederate generals reconnoitered Sheridan's camps from a towering aerie atop Massanutten Mountain and discovered that the Federals were strewn randomly across a wide stretch of rolling country north of Strasburg and Cedar Creek, with scant attention to tactical considerations. They hatched a daring plan.

General John B. Gordon led a long, stealthy, circuitous march along a trail so primitive that he called it "a pig's path." Gordon's column crossed the North Fork of the Shenandoah, crept across the nose of a mountain, and came back to the river opposite the unsuspecting left flank of Sheridan's force. At dawn on October 19, they splashed into the stream and dashed up the opposite slope into camps full of sleeping Yankees, screaming the chilling "Rebel Yell" as they ran. The onslaught routed the entire Federal VIII Corps. The Federal XIX Corps fought bravely for a time, but the momentum of the Southern surprise attack overwhelmed them too, and swept north to the vicinity of the village of Middletown.

Only the Federal VI Corps remained unassailed and unbroken. Together with the unhurt Northern cavalry, the VI Corps numbered as many men as Early's entire army, but staying the Rebels' momentum proved to be a difficult task. General Horatio G. Wright, commander of the corps, was acting as army commander that morning in Sheridan's absence. Wright deserves far more

As the winter of 1864–65 drew to a close, Petersburg's days as the last bastion of the Confederacy were starkly numbered. Federal thrusts farther and farther west to Burgess' Mill and Hatcher's Run had stretched Lee's lines impossibly thin. A final Confederate offensive at Fort Stedman on March 25 won brief, illusory success, before ending in a costly repulse. At Five Forks on April 1 and all around Petersburg on April 2 , Northern troops broke the Confederate line and forced the abandonment of the city. A desperate stand by a handful of Southern troops in Fort Gregg bought time for Lee's army to slip away and dash westward in a vain attempt to escape from Virginia and continue the war in North Carolina.

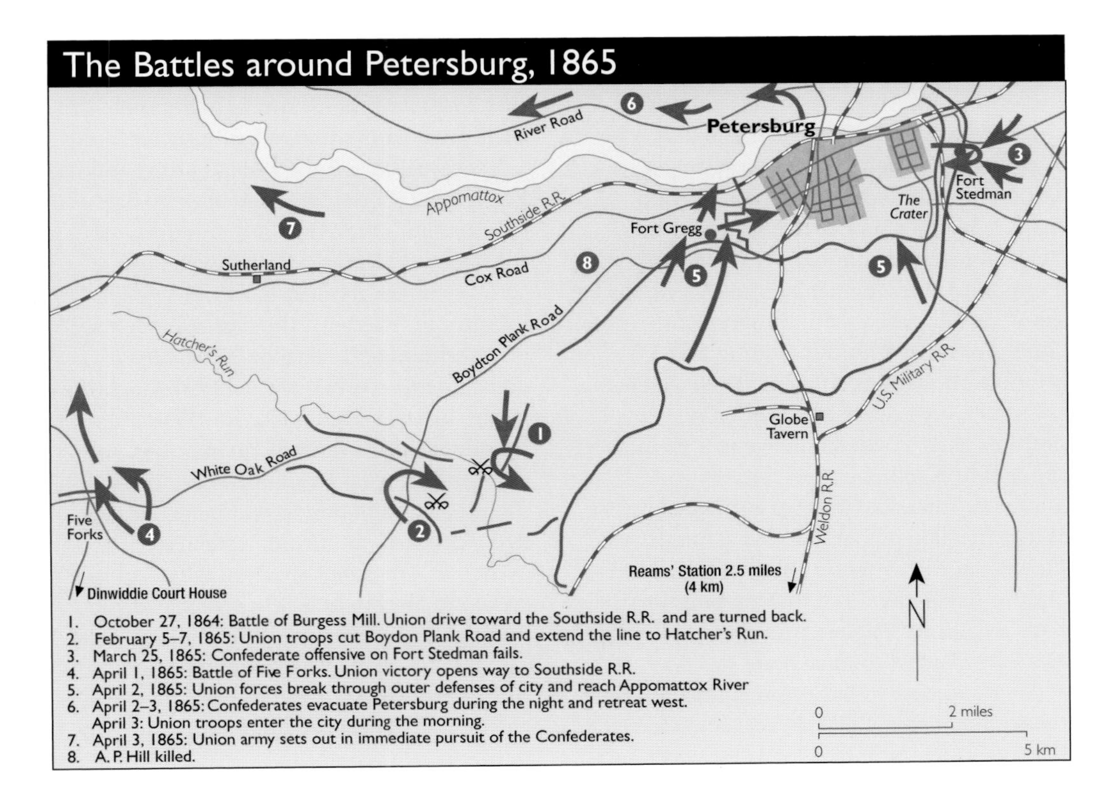

At dawn on October 19, 1864, Confederates dashed across the Shenandoah river and surprised camps full of sleeping Federals. For several hours they maintained their momentum and came near to winning the Battle of Cedar Creek despite being outnumbered more than three-to-one. (Public domain)

credit than he has been given for his calm, courageous stand that diluted Confederate momentum and restored the day for his army.

Early has received considerable blame for not pressing Wright more firmly to keep astride the momentum that was his only major advantage under the circumstances. The Confederate commander's quandary was compounded by the behavior of his troops: many of the weary, lean, hungry Southerners could not resist the array of food and booty in the captured camps. Their absence thinned Early's ranks and limited his options. Early's own summary to a member of his staff is telling: "The Yankees got whipped," he said, "and we got scared." When the aide prepared to leave for Richmond with a report, Early directed him "not to tell General Lee that we ought to have advanced" farther during the morning, "for ... we ought to have done so."

Sheridan dashed back from Winchester to the sound of the guns around Middletown, sent his immense force of cavalry sweeping around the Confederate left (for the third time in three battles), and advanced all across the line. With the momentum of the Southerners' surprise attack evaporated, there could be no doubt whatsoever about the outcome. Early's survivors fled south once more. All the bright hopes of the morning had vanished in the face of unchecked disaster. The Confederates had captured 20 cannon in their triumphant attack; now they lost all of them, and as many more of their own. Early's troops had inflicted 5,700 casualties on the Federal army, and lost 2,900 themselves. They also, by day's end, had for all intents and purposes lost the valley for the remainder of the war.

General Lee recalled most of Early's infantry to help with the desperate defense of Richmond and Petersburg. Cavalry detachments roamed the valley through the winter of 1864–65, raiding for the scant supplies available and harassing one another without major results. Both sides afflicted such of the civilian population as had not fled, and eked out a cold, bitter, costly existence. The small remnant with Early collapsed after only a faint struggle at the Battle of Waynesboro, in the southern valley, on March 2, 1865. The General himself was among the handful who escaped. By then, Lee's lines beyond the mountains were close to the breaking point.

From Richmond and Petersburg to Appomattox

Winter weather and its effect on a bad road system stymied Grant's steady probing westward toward the railroads through the war's last winter. The only major operation through that period unfolded on February 5–7, 1865 in the Battle of Hatcher's Run. Once again the Federals hoped to seize and hold the Boydton Plank Road; and once again they coveted the invaluable South Side Railroad, which ran just beyond the road. A strong Federal force moved into the area. It included II Corps, now under General Andrew A. Humphreys (long-time, much-admired corps commander Hancock had left the army), and Warren's V Corps returning to familiar ground.

On February 5, Humphreys battered Confederates who had hurried out from Petersburg. The next day, further Southern units swarmed over Warren and inflicted serious damage, but without lasting results. On the 7th, Lee concluded that he could not evict the Federals from their new perch, so both sides once more went back to entrenching. This latest extension of the line left Lee with 35 miles (56 km) to defend. About 1,500 Federals had fallen, and 1,000 Confederates.

General John B. Gordon entered service in 1861 without any military training or background whatsoever, but advanced steadily on merit until by the war's end he was among Lee's most important subordinates. Gordon designed and led the desperate attack on Fort Stedman on March 25, 1865. (Public domain)

Among the Southern casualties was General John Pegram. One contemporary remembered him fondly, if oddly as "a delightful & artistic whistler." The handsome young officer had been married in Richmond at St. Paul's Church on January 19 to Hetty Cary, a widely admired belle—"the most beautiful woman I ever saw in any land," enthused a Confederate officer. Five days later John celebrated his thirty-second birthday. Two more weeks and he was back at St. Paul's in a casket.

By mid-March, Lee's options had all but vanished. He accepted a desperate scheme hatched by the innovative General Gordon, back with the main army after leading the secret march at Cedar Creek in the Shenandoah Valley. Gordon would marshal as many men as could be spared from the

Confederate General John Pegram married a young woman acclaimed as among the most beautiful in the South, then was killed a few days later at Hatcher's Run. (Public domain)

Federals stand in review as their defeated foemen march past at Appomattox, en route to surrendering their arms. (Painting by Don Troiani, www.historicalartprints.com)

attenuated lines and lead them in a late-night assault against the Federals at Fort Stedman, not far from the Crater and on precisely the ground where the 1st Maine Heavy Artillery had been slaughtered the preceding June.

Careful planning and steady bravery brought Gordon initial success. Picked troops silently removed the defensive obstructions in front of the Confederate works opposite Stedman, then crawled up a ravine toward their enemy. Small detachments of volunteers silenced Federal pickets and deftly opened a corridor through the enemy obstacles near the fort. Storming parties followed and burst upon their surprised foe, capturing the fort and spreading down the line on either side. More Southern infantry followed, Gordon in their midst, to exploit the breakthrough.

A major Federal supply depot only a mile (1.6 km) behind Fort Stedman must have seemed to some of the starving Confederates to be the quintessential prize. Daylight brought stunning reality, however, as Federals farther down the lines on both sides brought artillery to bear. By 8:00 AM Yankees were swarming back toward Stedman. "The whole field was blue with them," a dismayed Southerner wrote. In the succinct summary of a disappointed North Carolinian, the fleeting success resembled a "meteor's flash that illumines for a moment and [then] leaves the night darker than before."

The Confederate horizon would darken even further during the next fortnight, then flicker out permanently. The advent of early spring gave Grant the chance to push west and southwest again. Lee obviously could not hold out much longer in Petersburg and Richmond, but the Federal commander feared that his wily adversary might find a way to slip away through the lines and head for North Carolina to join forces with another retreating Confederate army there.

Before Lee could attempt such a stratagem, his thinly manned lines snapped. Fighting by Union cavalry around Dinwiddie Court House on March 31 went well for Confederate General George E. Pickett, but to Lee's dismay Pickett fell back north to the invaluable Five Forks intersection on the White Oak Road. On April 1, Pickett, ever the dilettante, played host at a fish fry. Generals Fitzhugh Lee and Tom Rosser joined him at what became infamous as "The Shad Bake." While the generals enjoyed the respite from winter's short rations, Warren's diligent V Corps crashed into the exposed Confederate left and completely shattered it. Instead of applauding Warren's coup, Sheridan, commanding on the field, relieved him from command and assumed the mantle of the hero of Five Forks.

With Five Forks in Unionist hands, there remained nothing to keep them from the long-sought South Side Railroad. The next morning Grant ordered attacks all along the line and ended the siege of Petersburg. Horatio Wright's VI Corps rolled through A. P. Hill's troops almost at will. In a random encounter in the woods, two Federal enlisted men met Hill, who ranked behind only Longstreet among Lee's subordinates, accompanied only by a courier. After a nervous exchange of challenges, one Yankee fired a bullet that went through Hill's thumb and into his heart.

Farther northeast, closer to Petersburg, a tiny Confederate detachment held desperately to Fort Gregg to buy time for Lee to knit together a new line, and for the Confederate government to evacuate Richmond. Fort Gregg's defenders counted only two Mississippi regiments, one section of Louisiana artillery, and a handful of artillerists pressed into service as infantry—perhaps 300 men in all. The entire fresh Federal XXIV Corps attacked across an open field against the small work. Although it seemed to one witness that the Federal flags created "a solid line of bunting around the fort," the Southerners repulsed the first assault. Another fell back in confusion, leaving a bloody wake behind. Attacking Northerners wrote of "withering fire" that "mowed down our men most unmercifully." Finally the defenders collapsed under an overwhelming assault from all sides. They had shot more than 700 Federals. Only a handful of unwounded Southerners survived to be captured.

The sacrificial stand in Fort Gregg bought Lee time to protect Petersburg by means of a hastily connected interior line, but that night he had to abandon the city that for so long had been a focus of military operations in Virginia. For six days, April 3–8, 1865, Lee's Army of Northern Virginia wove a weary trail westward, hoping against hope to find a means of escape. Federal detachments, both infantry and cavalry, darted in and out of the desperate Southern columns, snaring prisoners and disrupting the retreat. Lee hoped to find rations for his men near Amelia Court House and Farmville; there were none. On April 6 the last pitched battle of the war in Virginia broke out on the banks of Sayler's Creek. The fighting did not rage hot or long. Federals closing in from three sides captured about 8,000 men, including eight general officers. Lee fought off pursuit at Cumberland Church on April 7 and kept heading west.

On the night of April 8, near Appomattox Court House, Lee found the enemy directly in his path as well as closing in from all sides. The next day he surrendered to Grant. The ceremony took place in the home of Wilmer McLean. By remarkable coincidence, four years earlier McLean had moved to Appomattox from his farm along Bull Run, to get away from the war that the Battle of Manassas had brought to his property. Not coincidentally, and entirely characteristically, Grant did not even invite Meade to the ceremony.

With four years of bloodshed at last ended in Virginia, other Confederate forces across the South faced imminent surrender. It now remained for Northerners to implement their hard-won victory, and for Southerners to find the means of sustenance in a destroyed country.

McHenry Howard's war

In September 1814, Francis Scott Key of Maryland wrote a poem as he watched British ships bombard Fort McHenry in the harbor of Baltimore. When an actor sang Key's "The Star-Spangled Banner" to the tune of an old drinking song, it at once became a popular patriotic air, and many years later the official national anthem of the United States.

Francis Scott Key's grandson, McHenry Howard, did not hesitate about going to war against the Star-Spangled Banner when Northern troops invaded his hometown of Baltimore in 1861. Federal authorities simply threw into jail those of Maryland's elected legislators who would not do as they were told. Howard and thousands of other young men from the state hurried southward, eager to fight for restoration of self-government. Their purpose, Howard wrote, was "not merely to aid the cause of the Confederacy as it was constituted, but believing that they were serving their own State—in subjection—in the only way that was left to them." Francis Scott Key had about 60 descendants living in 1860, and "every man, woman and child was Southern," Howard recalled, although "I cannot recall that any owned slaves in 1861."

When war interrupted Howard's civilian pursuits, he had been studying law after graduating from Princeton University. The 22-year-old lawyer in training belonged to a volunteer organization, the "Maryland Guard," that served purposes at least as much social as military. The guardsmen affected gorgeous uniforms of the "Zouave" variety, modeled after the outfits of French colonial troops who had caught the popular fancy in North America. Howard later described his garb with amusement provided by hindsight:

The full dress was a dark blue jacket, short and close fitting and much embroidered with yellow; a blue flannel shirt with a close row of small round gilt buttons (for ornament merely,) down the front, between yellow trimming; blue pantaloons, very baggy and gathered below the knee and falling over the tops of long drab gaiters; a small blue cap, of the kepi kind, also trimmed with yellow; and, finally, a wide red sash ... kept wide by hooks and eyes on the ends.

Private Howard would soon discover, in the world of a real soldier in the field, that "this gaudy dress, which made a very brilliant effect on street parade ... was totally unsuitable for any active service."

For nearly a year Howard served (more suitably attired, of course) in the ranks as an enlisted man with the 1st Maryland Infantry, Confederate States Army, made up of 1,000 young men who had escaped across the Potomac River to join the Southern cause. In the spring of 1862 he won a commission as lieutenant and aide-de-camp to fellow Marylander General Charles S. Winder. Lieutenant Howard remained at that lowest of the commissioned ranks for the final three years of the war. In his staff role, he had an opportunity to observe much of the conflict's most dramatic events, and many of its most significant leaders. After a Federal shell killed General Winder at Cedar Mountain in August 1862, Howard did staff duty with Generals Isaac R. Trimble, George H. Steuart, and George Washington Custis Lee, son of army commander General Robert E. Lee.

When Lee's Army of Northern Virginia headed north after the Battle of Chancellorsville, Lieutenant Howard followed as a supernumerary. His chief, General Trimble, had not reported back to the army after convalescing from a bad wound. That left Howard without a role, but he could not ignore his comrades' aggressive move northward and headed across country toward the Potomac to catch up with the army. When he splashed up the left bank of the river, the exiled Marylander noted sadly that it was the first time he had been on the soil of his native state in one month more than two years.

In Greencastle, Pennsylvania, Howard and a half-dozen other stray Confederates wound up in a hot street fight against mounted Yankees. Pistol bullets shattered windowpanes on all sides, dust obscured galloping horses, and the little band of Rebels had to flee. Later Howard and his mates chased a lone horseman for miles, only to discover that he was a Confederate major and an old friend.

During the army's subsequent retreat back toward Virginia, Howard rode through a Maryland town and thought wistfully, "Oh, that it was Baltimore!" On July 14, as the

McHenry Howard, 1838–1923. (Public domain)

Army of Northern Virginia abandoned Maryland, Howard wrote in his diary: "Feel very much depressed at the gloomy prospect for our State. I look around me constantly to see as much of it as I can before leaving it." As the army crossed the Potomac into Virginia, bandsmen gladly struck up "Sweet Home," but that seemed "a mockery" to the Marylanders. Howard "could not refrain from some bitter tears as I ... looked back to our beloved State."

For 10 months after Gettysburg, the exiled lieutenant performed staff duty under General George H. Steuart, a West Point graduate with "Old Army" ideas about organization and discipline. The summer after Gettysburg passed without a major engagement. During the lull, Howard and his mates fought against the elements and against logistical defects—just as has every army in every era. In September 1863, he wrote disgustedly in his diary: "Raining like

pitchforks—very disagreeable ... Regular equinoctial storm—have had nothing to eat for almost twenty-four hours." Violent downpours had drowned every fire for miles. Through one uncomfortable day, Lieutenant Howard, General Steuart, and three others huddled unhappily in a storm-shaken tent all day long, hungry and miserable.

Howard missed the campaigning around Bristoe Station in October 1863 because he had gone to the Confederate capital for religious reasons—to be confirmed in the Episcopal faith in Richmond's elegant St. Paul's Church. He had returned to duty by the time of the Battle of Mine Run, where his staff chores brought him under heavy fire: "the bullets coming through the switchy woods sounded somewhat like the hissing of a hail or sleet storm." He also noticed in that engagement one of the benchmarks of the war's evolution. Confederate soldiers had reached the conclusion that substantial protective fortifications made really good sense in the face of rifled musketry. They used "their bayonets, tin cups, and their hands, to loosen and scoop up the dirt, which was thrown on and around the trunks of old field pine trees" that they cut down and stretched lengthwise.

During the winter of 1863–64, genuine hardship became a constant companion of Southern soldiers. Lieutenant Howard described his diet, at a point in the food chain well above the privates and corporals, as consisting mostly of "corn dodgers"—corn meal cooked with water—for both breakfast and dinner. In good times, dinner also included "a soup made of water thickened with corn meal and mashed potatoes and cooked with a small piece of meat, which ... was taken out when the soup was done and kept to be cooked over again."

Events in the spring campaign in 1864 threw McHenry Howard into the cauldron of combat, then yanked him out of action as a prisoner of war. At the Wilderness, the night of May 5 echoed mordantly with the "moans and cries" of wounded men from both armies who lay between the lines and beyond succor. "In the still night air every groan could be heard," Howard wrote, "and the calls for water and entreaties to brothers and comrades by name to come and help them." The next morning, fires started in the underbrush by muzzle flashes spread through the Wilderness and burned to death some of the helpless wounded.

Spotsylvania followed Wilderness immediately. On May 10, 1864, a brutal

The burning of Richmond. (Ann Ronan Picture Library)

cross-fire caught and pinned down Howard and his friends. They had no option but to hug the ground and wait for darkness. "A more disagreeable half hour," he wrote in retrospect, "with a bullet striking a man lying on the ground every now and then, could not well have been spent." Two days later a Federal assault swept over the nose of the Confederate works near the point soon to be christened "the Bloody Angle." Yankee bayonets surrounded Howard and he went into a captivity that would last for six months. Howard's concise sketch map of the Angle at Spotsylvania remains an important artifact for studying the battle.

As his captors herded Lieutenant Howard to the rear at Spotsylvania, he began a prison experience shared by hundreds of thousands of Civil War soldiers. Howard wound up at Fort Delaware, in the middle of the Delaware River downstream from Philadelphia. There he enjoyed reasonably civilized treatment, by the uncivilized standards of the day. The fort's commander liked Howard and others of the Confederates, but some of his subordinates took the opportunity to abuse their power, as humans are wont to do. In November 1864, Howard went back south under a program for the exchange of prisoners. Once released in Georgia, he used a flask of brandy to bribe his way into a good railroad car on a Confederate train and by the end of 1864 had reached Richmond again.

Through the war's waning weeks, young Howard assisted General G. W. C. Lee in the effort to turn an accumulation of home-front troops, raw levies, and naval ratings into a hodge-podge brigade for emergency use. The emergency arose on April 2, 1865. The lieutenant was sitting in a pew at St Paul's, where he had been confirmed a few months earlier, for the 11:00 AM Sunday service, when a courier informed Jefferson Davis that the army's lines had been broken. Richmond must be abandoned. For four days the *ersatz* brigade under G. W. C. Lee took part in the retreat west and south from Richmond. In a mix-up that especially depressed and horrified Howard, the green troops loosed a volley against friends that killed several men, victims of mistaken friendly fire just a few hours before the army surrendered.

Howard fell into enemy hands again on April 6 at Sayler's Creek. This time his prison camp was Johnson's Island in Lake Erie. There he took the oath of allegiance to the United States on May 29 and made his long way home. Awaiting him in Baltimore was a demand, dated September 1862, that he report to Yankee conscript officers to be drafted into Federal service. Men had come to his mother's house and asked the names and occupations of all the family's males. McHenry's mother responded that her husband and eldest son were being held unconstitutionally as political prisoners in northern Bastilles. Four sons were serving in the Confederate army. "McHenry," she told her interrogators, was "with Stonewall Jackson and I expect he will be here soon." The officials wrote out the conscription demand and left. McHenry kept the souvenir the rest of his life.

Lieutenant Howard enjoyed a long and fruitful career after the war. He completed his legal training and practiced law in Baltimore for decades, finding time also to write extensively about his Confederate experiences. McHenry's lively, urbane recollections appeared in periodicals both North and South. He eventually turned his story into a charming and important—and sizable, at 423 pages—book that is a classic piece of Confederate literature: *Recollections of a Maryland Confederate Soldier and Staff Officer under Johnston, Jackson and Lee* (Baltimore: Williams & Wilkins Company, 1914). Howard died in his native Maryland on September 11, 1923, two months before his eighty-fifth birthday.

"This horrid and senseless war ..."

While soldiers carrying arms under both flags faced death or maiming at the battle front, their families at home coped with a wide variety of fundamental changes and challenges. Some home-front Americans met with fabulous economic opportunities; others with dire economic suffering. Millions of civilians struggled with numbing grief at the loss of loved ones, and millions more faced personal danger from scavengers—both "friendly" troops and invaders.

'The world around war" chapter of Gallagher, *The American Civil War,* describes those trends on a war-wide basis, including the impact of the war on the growth of government; women's roles in society and commerce; inflation and wages; speculation; corruption in the production of war materials; taxation; refugees; slavery and freed ex-slaves; and politics. In every context, the impact of the war upon civilians became broader and deeper during 1863–65 in the Virginia Theater than it had been during the war's first half.

Since all but a few days of the armies' campaigning in the theater unfolded on Confederate terrain, the impact on Southerners was far greater. Millions of Northern firesides mourned deeply and bitterly when the casualty lists from Virginia arrived, but on the economic and social front most Northern institutions actually gained strength, while the Confederacy was in the process of utter destruction. Southerners carefully watched the news about the price of gold in New York, and relished evidence of inflation. They were deluding themselves. The North thrived, as victorious nations' war economies generally do. Only on the battlefield could Confederates hope to create circumstances in which they might generate enough war-weariness to win their independence.

Southern civilians faced war's brutality on a far more intimate level than their quondam fellow-citizens in the North. Until fairly recently it had been conventional wisdom that mid-nineteenth-century mores kept occupying soldiery in check. A recent careful survey and indexing of United States Army courts-martial during the war has banished that old-fashioned notion. More than 83,000 Union soldiers came before courts. Nearly 5,000 of them were charged with crimes against civilians, including 558 for murder and 225 for rape. The number of formal trials, of course, only begins to reflect the volume of untried crimes, especially in areas where civilians were utterly powerless to protect themselves.

For millennia, European wars have trampled the citizens of the continent, shattering property and minds and leaving millions of non-combatant dead. In the two and a quarter centuries that comprise the relatively short life span of the United States however, no large body of American civilians has ever felt war's horrors up close—except Confederates during the final stages of the Civil War. As a direct result, soldiers from desolated areas of the South came under immense pressures to go home and protect their families. A letter from home came into evidence at a desertion trial of one of Lee's men. "I have always been proud of you," wrote Mary to Edward, "and since your connection with the Confederate army, I have been prouder of you than ever before ... but before God, Edward, unless you come home we must die." Edward went home. Provost guards brought him back to the army. After the trial Edward was returned to duty, perhaps on the strength of the emotions provoked by the letter. Soon thereafter he was killed in action.

Margaret Junkin Preston, whose condolence letter to a stricken friend was one of many millions written during the American Civil War. (Virginia Military Institute Museum)

The personal suffering and loss would gradually heal in many instances, but the destruction of more than 620,000 lives could not be erased. Margaret Junkin Preston, one of the leading female authors in the country, wrote a condolence letter to a friend whose brother had just fallen victim to what Preston called "this horrid and senseless war." Maggie's heart-felt emotions capture what so many millions of others went through.

I cannot refrain from mingling my grief with yours … It is dreadful to have our loved ones die … [We are] utterly shaken by the uncontrollable outthrusting of our mere human grief at seeing the pleasant face never never more … the tender eyes shut, not to be opened again—the sweet interchange of thought, feelings, emotions—all all over! … The Blessed God comfort you under this sense of loss which will press upon you so agonizingly.

A few weeks after she wrote this tender letter, Maggie faced the same ordeal when her own 17-year-old stepson fell mortally wounded in action.

Ella Washington and the Federal Army

George Armstrong Custer became forever famous when he led more than 250 cavalrymen to annihilation on the Little Big Horn River in 1876. A dozen years earlier he had been infamous among Virginians for destruction of civilian property and executing prisoners. Before either of those notable episodes of Custer's life and death, he had been the gallant savior of a hard-beset Virginian woman who lived near Richmond.

Ella Bassett grew up on her father's sizable plantation "Clover Lea," a dozen miles northeast of Virginia's capital city. She had been born in September 1834 at another family estate, "Eltham," in New Kent County. In May 1862, the Civil War came to Eltham, and the next month it washed up on the grounds of Clover Lea as well. Two years later the war, by then a hard-eyed, unforgiving monster, descended on Clover Lea in an episode fraught with terror for Ella. Her descriptions of the ordeal she experienced in May and June 1864 serve as an example in microcosm of the suffering of hundreds of thousands of civilians at the mercy of invading troops.

By 1864, Ella had been a married woman for 3 years. Her husband, Colonel Lewis

Ella Bassett Washington, 1834–98. (Courtesy of the Mount Vernon Ladies' Association)

Washington, was a direct descendant of the first President, George Washington (through George's wife and family; he had no natural children). So was Ella. She and Lewis each had ancestry back to the first President's family on both sides of their own parentage, and accordingly Lewis and Ella were themselves distant cousins by multiple connections. Lewis was more than two decades older than Ella and had been married before. Ella evidently had little or nothing to do with his two daughters, who lived with relatives in Maryland, but she was fond of stepson James Barroll Washington.

The war's preliminaries had fallen on Lewis Washington with alarming savagery the year before he married Ella. On an October morning in 1859, several men used a fence rail to batter down the door of Washington's home, "Beall Air," near Harpers Ferry, Virginia. The intruders—a detachment from the marauding party directed by John Brown—knew that Lewis owned relics of George Washington and demanded them as booty. They carried Lewis off as a hostage. He witnessed, as a prisoner, the storming by United States Marines of Brown's hideout at Harpers Ferry. Directing the storming party was Colonel Robert E. Lee, United States Army. Among the first men to the door of the stronghold was Lieutenant J. E. B. Stuart, United States Army, acting as an aide to Lee.

The year after Lewis's brief ordeal at the hands of Brown's merry band, his new bride, cousin Ella, moved into Beall Air. In late 1861, the couple moved from Beall Air to Ella's family place at Clover Lea. She attributed the need to relocate to "the critical condition of my health." Since Lewis's home stood in a mountainous region, and Clover Lea plantation lay in the relatively swampy ground near Richmond, contemporary notions would have suggested (not inaccurately) that health considerations would actually militate in favor of Beall Air. Perhaps Ella's concern was to be near her own family to secure their assistance. Not long after the Washingtons relocated to Clover Lea, their baby daughter Betty died. In June 1863, Ella bore a son, William D. Washington.

The 1862 campaign around Richmond nearly resulted in the capture of the Confederate capital and an early end to the war. Fortunately for the Southern army, its timid commander fell wounded at the end of May and General R. E. Lee assumed command. In a week of fighting denominated the "Seven Days' Campaign," Lee slowly and at great cost drove away the besieging Northerners and bottled them up against the James River. Lee won the week's biggest battle with the largest charge he ever launched during the war, at Gaines' Mill, just five miles (8 km) from Clover Lea.

In the aftermath, suffering wounded men clogged the entire countryside. A major hospital mushroomed next to the Bassett-Washington property. The Richmond *Whig*

"Clover Lea," home of Ella Bassett Washington, photographed in the 1930s. (Author's collection)

three times published appreciative notices of the kindness bestowed on sick and wounded soldiers by women of the neighborhood, "especially ... the ladies of 'Clover Lea.'" A few weeks later, the same newspaper reported the death of baby Betty. It is hard to avoid the speculation (but impossible to prove) that microbes from the hundreds of sick, wounded, and infected soldiers convalescing in the vicinity might have brought on the infant's demise.

Although the Federals failed to capture Richmond during that spring of 1862, they did capture Ella's stepson, Lieutenant James Washington. The youngster, who had been serving on the staff of Confederate army commander Joseph E. Johnston, found himself in the hands of a friend from West Point days, George A. Custer. The quondam classmate treated Washington to a cigar and something to drink, and rounded up some other friends serving in the Union army. That evening, Ella wrote later, the prisoner and his captors enjoyed "rather a jollification in one of the headquarters tents," reminiscing about their cadet days at the famous Benny Haven's Tavern near the military academy grounds.

When the provost guard took young Washington away to head for a prisoner-of-war camp, Custer stuffed some US currency in his friend's vest pocket to help smooth his captivity. "You must have some money, Jim," Custer said, "those pictures in your pockets [Confederate currency] don't pass up there." The cartel for exchange of prisoners had not yet broken down at that stage, so James went back to Confederate service upon exchange after a short period in captivity. Two years later, George Custer would be in a position to help James Washington's stepmother in a more substantial fashion.

War's mailed fist went rampaging northward for nearly two years after the

fighting around Richmond in May and June 1862—but in May 1864 hostile troops swept across the grounds of Clover Lea and threatened to destroy everything that the Bassetts and Washingtons owned. On May 28, Ella could hear rifles rattling in the near distance. It was a time "of dreadful suspense and anxiety." She wondered in her diary that evening whether her brothers had been in the fighting, and whether they had survived. A few Confederates galloped past, pausing only briefly. "God bless you, boys," Ella's father said as they hurried away. As their horses' hoofbeats faded, Ella thought they left behind "a strange silence, brooding over nature like a pall."

The next morning, after a terrified night and little sleep, Ella had to face the invasion of her property by swarms of uncontrolled enemy foragers. This "most horrible set of creatures I ever saw" took everything in sight and made the women fear for their safety. Ella longed for a guillotine to "take their heads off in just as rapid a style" as they were killing the farm animals.

In desperation, Ella Washington sent notes off to her stepson's friend, General Custer, hoping that he might come to assist her. One of the messages did reach the Federal cavalry general and on the 30th he arrived in person at Clover Lea, where he at once promised to protect the stepmother of his friend James Washington, and her property. Custer behaved gallantly with the pretty Virginian, who despite being his school chum's stepmother was not much beyond his own age. Ella wrote of the pleasure of finding someone, in the midst of "this host of enemies, with whom we can feel some human sympathy."

Even though they enjoyed intermittent protection afforded by the connection with Custer, Clover Lea and its civilians still suffered under the hostile occupation. Despite her gratitude for Custer's aid, Ella told her diary: "In wickedness and impudence no nation ever equalled the Yankees." Years later, in contrast, she still wrote warmly of the enemy general's "generous and kindly deeds done under trying circumstances."

Mrs. Washington's experience as a helpless pawn on the chessboard of war was of a kind shared by countless thousands of other women. Her own vivid words describe some of what she saw and felt:

the dreadful Yankees ... I feel so much fatigued I can scarcely dress ... What a day of horrors and agony, may I never spend such another ... The demon of destruction [was] at [our] very door, surrounding, swallowing [us] up in its fearful scenes of strife ... How can such an army of devils not human beings ever succeed? ... I fancied (though it seems a very ridiculous idea) that there was something almost human in [the dying farm animals'] screaming voices ... I was glad when the last had been killed ... I am feeling physically and mentally oppressed, never found my nerves so shaken, and my courage so tried.

As General Custer took his leave of Clover Lea and went back to war, Ella described to him the frustration of being helpless to affect her own fate. "You men don't know how much more intolerable the martyrdom of endurance is than the martyrdom of action." "Some of us," he replied, "can comprehend, and sympathize, too. War is a hard, cruel, terrible thing. Men must fight, and women weep." Ella gave Custer as a token of her appreciation a button from George Washington's coat. The General set the button as a brooch and presented it to his wife, who eventually donated the relic to the US Military Academy. It survives today in the collection of Custer Battlefield National Monument, Montana.

Custer subsequently played a role in making war "a hard, cruel, terrible thing" in the Shenandoah Valley. In September, his troopers murdered six Confederate prisoners in a churchyard and the streets of Front Royal. One was a 17-year-old youngster whose widowed mother screamed in horror as she pleaded in vain for his life. A girl in the village wrote of how that "dark day of 1864 ... clouded my childhood" and haunted her dreams forever. The famed Confederate partisan leader John S. Mosby ordered execution of a like number of Custer's captive men, but the Southerners blanched after carrying out half of the brutal job and let the rest go. Twelve years later, Custer himself died with scores of his troopers at the Battle of the Little Bighorn.

James Barroll Washington became a railroad president after the war and died in 1900. His father, Ella's husband, died in 1871, leaving the widow without many resources. Ella used her Washington connections to assist ex-Confederates in procuring Federal pardons after the war. When that lucrative but short-term business died down, she subsided into genteel poverty and died in New York in 1898.

Lieutenant James Barroll Washington and Captain George Armstrong Custer in 1862, while Washington was a prisoner of war in the keeping of his old friend from the US Military Academy. (Little Bighorn Battlefield National Monument, National Park Service)

From Appomattox to Liverpool

Lee's surrender at Appomattox Court House on April 9, 1865 essentially ended the war in the Virginia Theater. Many thousands of men had slipped out of the weary, retreating, Confederate column as the cause became patently hopeless, thus escaping the final surrender. Some of those soldiers attempted to head south into North Carolina to join the Southern army still fighting there under General Joseph E. Johnston. That forlorn hope evaporated when Johnston surrendered to General William T. Sherman near Durham Station on April 26, after complicated negotiations involving Washington politicians.

In the weeks that followed, Confederates who had not signed paroles at either Appomattox or Durham Station gradually made their way to occupied towns and took the oath of allegiance to the United States. Some troops from the deep South took weeks or even months to reach homes, many of them desolated, in Alabama or Louisiana or Texas. Soldiers who surrendered with Lee, or took the oath separately later, missed the ordeal suffered by their comrades who had been taken prisoner just a few hours before the Appomattox ceremony. Confederates captured during the retreat from Richmond and Petersburg, including thousands of men who surrendered at Sayler's Creek, went off to prison camps as though the war still raged on. Most did not secure their freedom until mid-June 1865.

Meanwhile, the triumphant Federal armies converged on the national capital for a mass celebration of the war's end. On May 23 and 24, hundreds of thousands of blue-uniformed veterans marched in serried ranks. As the victorious divisions and brigades and regiments began to muster out of service, far-flung Confederate detachments continued to fight forlornly, and finally to give up the struggle. On June 2, General E. Kirby Smith formally accepted terms at Galveston, Texas, and surrendered the Confederate forces in the Trans-Mississippi. Weeks later the Confederate cruiser CSS *Shenandoah* was still capturing whalers in the Bering Sea. Lieutenant James I. Waddell, CSN, finally surrendered the *Shenandoah* to British officials at Liverpool on November 6, 1865.

The reconstruction of the desolated Southern states remained to be done, and the healing of divisions, and the reunion of the United States in fact as well as in law. None of those tasks would be easy; nor could they be accomplished to the satisfaction of everyone.

Recovery and reconstruction

Fighting in the American Civil War included more than 10,000 recorded battles, engagements, and skirmishes. Virginia served as the stage for more of those than any other state—some 2,200; Tennessee ranked next with about 1,500. At least 620,000 soldiers and sailors died during the war, more than 365,000 of them Federals. Microbes wreaked more havoc than bullets did, in an age of primitive notions regarding sanitation and medical science. Postwar calculations by the Federal Surgeon General, for instance, tabulated 45,000 Northern deaths from dysentery and diarrhea; 20,000 from pneumonia; and more than 9,000 by drowning or other non-battle accidents.

Political consequences of the conflict wrought fundamental changes in the nature

Defeated Confederates went home to face an ordeal of a different sort in a shattered land bereft of food and sustenance. Military Reconstruction lasted more than a decade in some places in the South. (Public domain)

The Last Days of War, April 1865

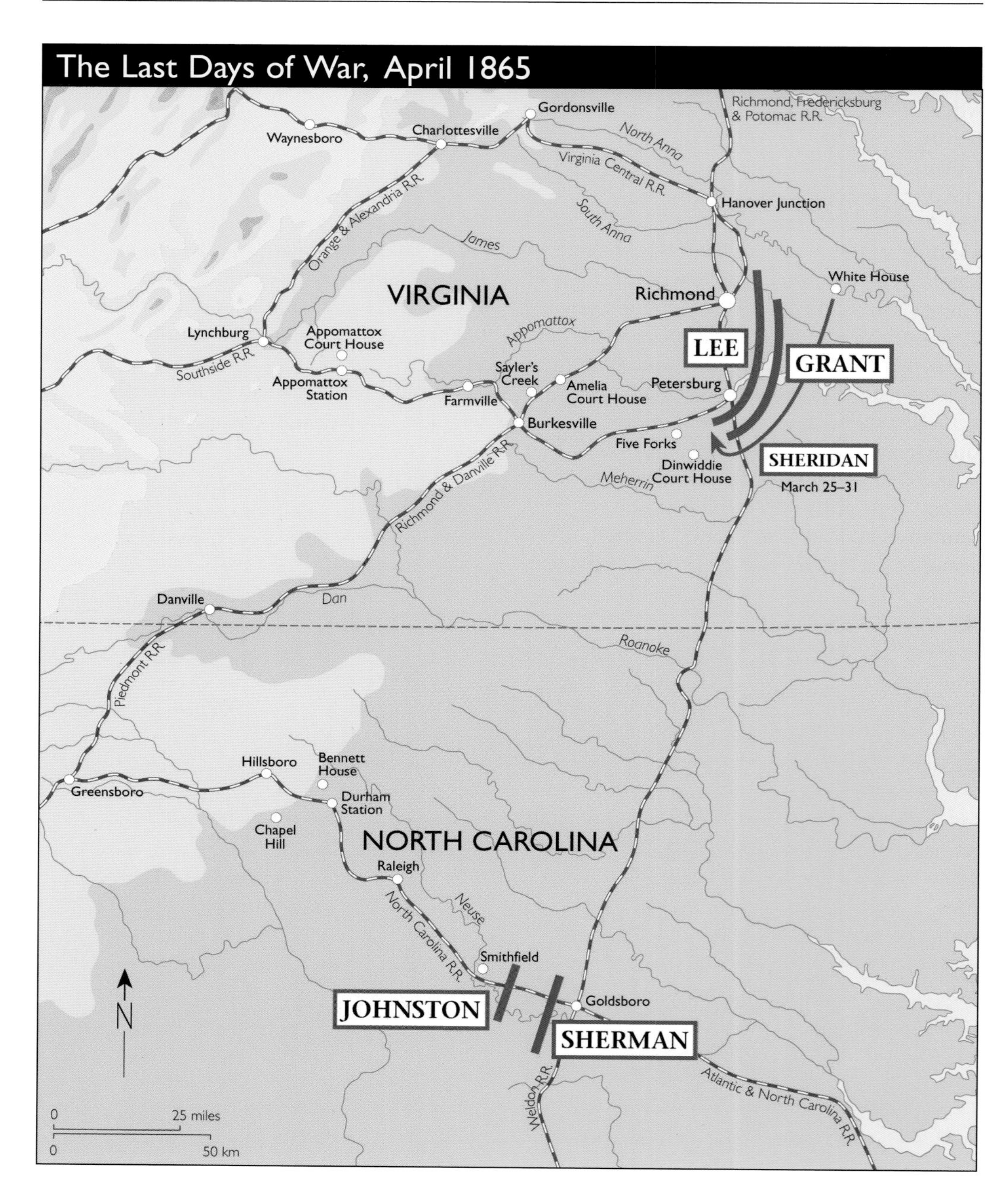

When Lee's attenuated lines around Petersburg finally snapped at the beginning of April, he hoped to slip west along the railroad, then turn south to join the Confederate army in North Carolina under General Joseph E. Johnston. Federal columns hounded the Southern remnants on all sides. At Appomattox Court House on April 8, Lee found a substantial force of the enemy in front of him, eliminating his last hope of escape. He surrendered the next day. Johnston did likewise on April 26 at Durham Station, North Carolina, effectively ending the war in the Virginia Theater.

of institutions and culture in North America. The results of the war ensured prompt freedom for some 3.5 million black slaves, and also opened an entirely new chapter of restructuring American society and economy. Triumphant Northern politicians had the opportunity to remake the South in their own image, and for their own purposes, in the Reconstruction era.

Perhaps the most significant event in that process came just five days after Appomattox when pro-Confederate actor John Wilkes Booth assassinated President Abraham Lincoln at Ford's Theater in Washington. Lincoln's death removed his pragmatic, conciliatory influence and left control in the hands of radical politicians of vindictive temper. The President of Harvard University sounded a prevailing tone when he declared, "The task for the North is to spread knowledge and culture over the regions that sit in darkness." On a more visceral level, anti-Confederate activists such as the Rev. James W. Hunnicutt advocated violence: "The white men have houses and lands ... you can apply the torch to the dwellings of your enemies ... the boy of ten and the girl of twelve can apply the torch." Considerable political and racial violence swept the desolated South.

With virtually every local citizen banned from office as a conquered rebel, Southern states fell under the control of venturesome Northerners who came south with little luggage but a carpetbag (a traveling bag made of carpeting), and who came to be known colloquially as "carpetbaggers." Some surely brought with them altruistic agendas; others surely came to loot from prostrate and powerless individuals and localities. General John M. Schofield, a veteran Union officer assigned to duty in postwar Virginia, called the eager immigrants "ignorant or unprincipled" and summarized their behavior in a letter to U. S. Grant: "They could only hope to obtain office by disqualifying everybody in the state who is capable of discharging official duties, and all else to them was of comparatively slight importance."

The ruling political bloc in Washington welcomed the vacuum. Congressman Thaddeus Stevens of Pennsylvania summarized his goals succinctly: "Unless the rebel States ... should be made republican in spirit, and placed under the guardianship of loyal men, all our blood and treasure will have been spent in vain." A Federal soldier stationed in Alabama expressed his view of the Southerners in his power: "There is not 9 out of 10 of these so called 'Whiped' traitors that I would trust until I saw the rope applied to their Necks, then I would only have Faith in the quality of the rope." The carpetbag Governor of South Carolina (the last state returned to home rule) defended the record of his administration, insisting that he had observed "steady progress toward good government, purity of administration, reform of abuses, and the choice of capable and honest public officers in those States in which the colored race had the most complete control."

Southerners powerless under carpetbag government faced concerns far more basic than political institutions. A quest for food and shelter and minimal financial security ruled their lives in a barren land reduced to ashes. A 28-year-old woman living in central Virginia described her feelings in a letter to her sister written in August 1865. The entire region had been "reduced almost to indigence ... I sometimes feel as if it could not be reality, and that I have been the victim of some hideous nightmare." Returning survivors from the army were so "heart broken" that it "wrung your very soul." She hoped that somehow the fight might be renewed. Feeling against the North was "intense ... It will never pass away." The distraught woman closed her letter by expressing the hope that small children would be taught to "Fear God, love the South, and *live to avenge her.*" In 1867 a former Confederate colonel wrote with bitter nostalgia of "that blissful time, for the return of which I most devoutly pray, when it was lawful to kill Yankees."

Virginia completed Reconstruction before most other ex-Confederate states, seating representatives in Washington in January 1870 who had been elected by broad popular vote. The North meanwhile enjoyed a fabulous explosion in wealth, fed by the war's profits and building upon industrialization generated by war contracts. As a direct consequence, hundreds of thousands of Southerners emigrated north for work or west for fresh opportunities on the frontier.

For the first time in United States history, veterans became a basic force in politics. Northern veterans touted their honorable service in what came to be known as "waving the bloody shirt." In Virginia, political pundits noticed that it was almost impossible to be elected governor without the stigmata of a visible war wound. Union veterans lobbied for National Cemeteries, the first in the country's history, and especially for pensions. Federals with any sort of disability drew pensions from Washington. As a byproduct, books full of memoirs of horrors suffered in Southern prisons began to appear. They soon blossomed into a virtual cottage industry. Most included significant exaggerations; some contained not even a kernel of truth.

Pensions for all veterans followed. Southern survivors, of course, had no access to benefits from the Federal government, so their states inaugurated local pension systems. Virginia pensions began under an Act dated 1888. Subsequent laws in 1900 and 1902 expanded coverage. Civil War pensions marked the first large-scale government welfare system in the country's history. By the 1920s and beyond, pensions had become so attractive during the Great Depression that fraudulent applications abounded. Recent scholarship that examined the stories of the final 10 self-announced survivors of the war (five from each side) discovered that every one of them was entirely bogus.

The war resulted in a revolution in North American medical practices. European scientists such as Pasteur and Lister had been making strides in germ theory and antiseptic practice. Americans caring for their millions of soldiers gradually absorbed some of that important new technique. Hard experience produced other empirical changes in treatment.

Military art and science underwent an even more profound evolution. The Civil War was the first major conflict in which: most participants used rifled shoulder arms; percussion caps replaced less efficient ignition systems; railroads played a major role, both logistically and strategically, with dramatic increases in army mobility; field entrenchments became (by 1864) a routine but significant defensive mechanism; ironclad warships ruled naval affairs; general-staff functions began to receive adequate attention; telegraphy was used; standardization of production became effective (in the North); and some soldiers (almost exclusively Federals) employed repeating weapons and breech-loaders. The contending armies began the war employing techniques akin to those of the Napoleonic Wars. By 1865, combat was being waged in a manner that foreshadowed the First World War. Only the following year, Prussia was employing a skilled general staff, the telegraph, rifled arms, and a thoroughly planned railroad network, together with the other new features of warfare, to crush the Austrians. The Civil War had initiated a wide array of changes in the conduct of war that was to dominate battlefields for the next 60 years.

Glossary

abattoir A slaughterhouse.
agrarian Rural, or relating to agriculture.
amour-propre Self respect or self-esteem.
artillery Cannon and other large weapons capable of firing ammunition.
breastwork A kind of temporary defense or fortification, such as a trench.
bulwark A structure, such as a wall or a mound of earth, that is built to protect against an attack or other danger.
cadre A group of people with special skills or training who are put in control of others.
calumny A false statement intended to harm someone's reputation.
canister A kind of ammunition designed to scatter when fired from a cannon.
cavalry Soldiers that are trained to fight on horseback.
infantry Soldiers that fight on foot.
maelstrom A powerful and chaotic vortex.
materiel Military supplies and equipment.
nom de guerre A nickname or pseudonym used in battle.
opprobrium Public reproach or shame.
pacifist A person who is opposed to war and violence.
quondam Former.
rodomontade Bragging or boasting.
siege A battle tactic in which an attacking army blockades or isolates their opponent.
swath A broad strip.
vassal A person who is allowed to use land in exchange for being subservient to a superior authority.

For more information

American Battlefield Preservation Program
1201 Eye Street NW 2255
Washington, DC 20005
(202) 354-2069
Web site: http://www.nps.gov/history/hps/abpp
A part of the National Park Service, the American Battlefield Preservation Program is dedicated to protecting American battlefields and raising awareness about battlefield preservation.

American Civil War Museum
297 Steinwehr Avenue
Gettysburg, PA 17325-2815
(717) 334-6245
Web site: http://www.gettysburgmuseum.com
Located in Gettysburg, Pennsylvania, this museum contains numerous exhibits related to the Civil War.

Civil War Preservation Trust
1156 15th Street NW
Suite 900
Washington, D.C. 20005
(202) 367-1861
Web site: http://civilwar.org

This nonprofit organization works to preserve Civil War battlefields.

Gettysburg National Military Park
1195 Baltimore Pike, Suite 100
Gettysburg, Pennsylvania 17325
(717) 334-1124 ext. 8023
Web Site: http://www.nps.gov/gett/index.htm
Today, the Gettysburg battlefield is now a national park that draws many visitors each year.

National Civil War Museum
One Lincoln Circle at Reservoir Park
Harrisburg, PA 17103
(717) 260-1861
Web site: http://www.nationalcivilwarmuseum.org/index_1.php
The National Civil War Museum has a vast collection of artifacts, documents, and photographs from the Civil War era.

Smithsonian National Museum of American History
1400 Constitution Ave NW
Washington, DC 20004
(202) 633-1000
Web site: http://americanhistory.si.edu
Located in Washington, D.C., this museum has a wide-ranging collection of artifacts from American history, including many from the Civil War. It also has numerous exhibits and educational programs for visitors.

Web sites

Due to the changing nature of Internet links, Rosen Publishing has developed an online list of Web sites related to the subject of this book. This site is updated regularly. Please use this link to access the list:

http://www.rosenlinks.com/cweh/eastb

For further reading

Blount, Roy Jr. *Robert E. Lee: A Life*. New York, NY: Penguin, 2006.

Bunting, Josiah. *Ulysses S. Grant*. New York, NY: Times Books, 2004.

Foote, Shelby. *Stars in Their Courses: The Gettysburg Campaign June–July 1863*. New York, NY: Modern Library, 1994.

Golay, Michael. *Civil War*. New York, NY: Chelsea House, 2010.

Grant, Ulysses S. *Ulysses S. Grant: Memoirs and Selected Letters*. New York, NY: Library of America, 1990.

Krick, Robert K. *Stonewall Jackson at Cedar Mountain*. Chapel Hill, NC: University of North Carolina Press, 1990.

McPherson, James M. *Abraham Lincoln*. New York, NY: Oxford University Press, 2009.

McPherson, James M. *Battle Cry of Freedom: The Civil War Era*. New York, NY: Oxford University Press, 2003.

McPherson, James M. *Hallowed Ground: A Walk at Gettysburg*. New York, NY: Crown Journeys, 2003.

McPherson, James M., and James K. Hogue. *Ordeal by Fire: The Civil War and Reconstruction*. Boston, MA: McGraw-Hill, 2009.

Mrazek, Robert J. *Stonewall's Gold*. New York, NY: St. Martin's Press, 1999.

Olson, Steven P. *Lincoln's Gettysburg Address: A Primary Source Investigation*. New York, NY: Rosen Publishing, 2004.
Sears, Stephen W. *Gettysburg*. New York, NY: Houghton Mifflin, 2004.
Shaara, Michael. *The Killer Angels: A Novel of the Civil War*. New York, NY: Modern Library, 2004.
Sheridan, Philip H. *Personal Memoirs of P.H. Sheridan*. New York, NY: Barnes and Noble, 2006.
Wallenfeldt, Jeff, Ed. *The American Civil War and Reconstruction: People, Politics, and Power*. New York, NY: Britannica Educational Publishing and Rosen Educational Services, 2010.
Wert, Jeffry D. *Cavalryman of the Lost Cause: A Biography of J. E. B. Stuart*. New York, NY: Simon & Schuster, 2008.
Whittle, William C., Jr.; D. Alan Harris and Anne B. Harris, eds. *The Voyage of the CSS Shenandoah: A Memorable Cruise*. Tuscaloosa, AL: University of Alabama Press, 2005.
Wittenberg, Eric J. *General James Longstreet: The Confederacy's Most Controversial Soldier*. New York, NY: Simon & Schuster, 1993.

Bibliography

Primary sources

Brown, Varina Davis (ed.), *A Colonel at Gettysburg and Spotsylvania*, Columbia, South Carolina, 1931.
Chesnut, Mary Boykin, *A Diary from Dixie*, New York, 1905.
Grant, Ulysses S., *Personal Memoirs of U. S. Grant*, 2 vols, New York, 1886.
Holt, David, *A Mississippi Rebel in the Army of Northern Virginia*, Baton Rouge, Louisiana, 1995.
Lee, R. E., *The Wartime Papers of R. E. Lee*, Boston, Massachusetts, 1961.
McClure, A. K. (ed.), The *Annals of the War Written by Leading Participants North and South*, Philadelphia, Pennsylvania, 1879.
Meade, George Gordon, Jr, *The Life and Letters of George Gordon Meade*, 2 vols, New York, 1913.
Wainwright, Charles S., *A Diary of Battle*, New York, 1962.
Worsham, John H., *One of Jackson's Foot Cavalry*, New York, 1912.

Secondary sources

Catton, Bruce, *A Stillness at Appomattox*, New York, 1953.
Coddington, Edwin B., *The Gettysburg Campaign*, New York, 1968.
Davis, William C., *The Battle of New Market*, Garden City, New York, 1975.
Dowdey, Clifford, *Lee's Last Campaign*, Boston, Massachusetts, 1960.
Dyer, Frederick H., *A Compendium of the War of the Rebellion*, Des Moines, Iowa, 1908.
Freeman, Douglas S., *Lee's Lieutenants*, 3 vols, New York, 1942–44.
Furgurson, Ernest B., *Not War But Murder: Cold Harbor 1864*, New York, 2000.
Gallagher, Gary W. (ed.), *The Spotsylvania Campaign*, Chapel Hill, North Carolina, and London, 1998.

Gallagher, Gary W. (ed.), *Three Days at Gettysburg: Essays on Confederate and Union Leadership*, Kent, Ohio, and London, 1999.
Hattaway, Herman, and Archer Jones, *How the North Won: A Military History of the Civil War*, Urbana, Illinois, 1983.
Henderson, G. F. R., *The Science of War*, London, 1905.
Humphreys, Andrew A., *The Virginia Campaign of '64 and '65: The Army of the Potomac and the Army of the James*, New York, 1883.
Johnson, Ludwell H., *Division and Reunion: America, 1848–1877*, New York, 1978.
Marvel, William, *A Place Called Appomattox*, Chapel Hill, North Carolina, and London, 2000.
McPherson, James M., *Battle Cry of Freedom: The Civil War Era*, New York, 1988.
Pfanz, Harry W., *Gettysburg: Culp's Hill and Cemetery Hill*, Chapel Hill, North Carolina, and London, 1993.
Pfanz, Harry W., *Gettysburg: The Second Day*, Chapel Hill, Northern Carolina, and London, 1987.
Rhea, Gordon C., *The Battle of the Wilderness*, Baton Rouge, Louisiana, 1994.
Rogers, H. C. B., *The Confederates and Federals at War*, London, 1973.
Trudeau, Noah Andre, *The Last Citadel: Petersburg*, Boston, Massachusetts, 1991.
Warren, Robert Penn, *The Legacy of the Civil War*, New York, 1964.
Wert, Jeffry D., *From Winchester to Cedar Creek: The Shenandoah Campaign of 1864*, Carlisle, Pennsylvania, 1987.
Wiley, Bell I., *Confederate Women*, Westport, Connecticut, and London, 1975.
Wilson, Edmund, *Patriotic Gore: Studies in the Literature of the American Civil War*, New York, 1962.

Index

About the authors

Professor Robert O'Neill, AO D.Phil, is the Chichele Professor of the History of War at the University of Oxford. His wealth of knowledge and expertise shapes the series content and provides up-to-the-minute research and theory. Born in 1936 an Australian citizen, he served in the Australian army (1955–68) and has held a number of eminent positions in history circles. He has been Chichele Professor of the History of War and a Fellow of All Souls College, Oxford, since 1987. He is the author of many books including works on the German army and the Nazi party, and the Korean and Vietnam Wars.

Robert K. Krick was born in California and has been responsible for the preservation of several battlefields in Virginia for more than 30 years. He is the author of a dozen books and more than 100 published articles. His *Stonewall Jackson at Cedar Mountain* won the Douglas Southall Freeman Award for Best Book in Southern History.